KT-179-297

EXPLORING PLAY
IN THE
PRIMARY CLASSROOM

Gill Beardsley
with
Penelope Harnett

David Fulton Publishers
London

David Fulton Publishers Ltd
Ormond House, 26–27 Boswell Street, London WC1N 3JD

First published in Great Britain by David Fulton Publishers 1998

Note: The right of Gill Beardsley and Penelope Harnett to be identified as the authors of this work has been asserted by them in accordance with the Copyright, Designs and Patents Act 1988.

British Library Cataloguing in Publication Data
A catalogue record for this book is available from the British Library

ISBN 1–85346–463–5

Typeset by Helen Skelton, London
Printed in Great Britain by BPC Books and Journals Ltd, Exeter

Contents

Acknowledgements

It is with pleasure that we wish to thank Mary Jane Drummond and Andrew Pollard for their original encouragement and support of the writing of this book, and their helpful reading and advice.

We also gratefully acknowledge the contributions of the students and teachers who have spent time discussing their practice with us. In particular we would like to thank the staff and pupils of: Coniston Infants School; Eastcombe Primary School; Henleaze Junior School; May Park Primary School; Redcliffe Nursery School; Westbury Park Primary School; and Willow Green Infant School.

We thank Dorset County Council AVA Centre for the use of excerpts from their video *Cardboard Boxes and Other Things*, and the High/Scope Foundation for giving permission to reproduce the table on page 32. A number of individuals have also generously given their time in helping us to discuss and clarify our ideas. These include Mary Blight and Sue Cook from Redcliffe Nursery School; Mary Eccleston; Patricia Chubb; Maggie Kirby; Sylvia Dodd; Jane Fitzgerald; Yvonne Chivers; Jennie Brislen. Peter Harnett has always given us encouragement and above all made it possible for us to have time to talk. But, more than anyone, we should thank Philip, aged seven, aided and abetted by his brother Timothy, a master player, whose imagination and enthusiasm for pretend play sustained us throughout.

Gill Beardsley and Penelope Harnett
Bristol
September 1998

Case Studies

The Primary Curriculum Series

This innovative series is an ideal means of supporting professional practice in the post-Dearing era, when a new focus on the quality of teaching and learning is possible. The series promotes reflexive teaching and active forms of pupil learning. The books explore the implications of these commitments for curriculum and curriculum-related issues.

The argument of each book flows in, around and among a variety of case studies of classroom practice, introducing them, probing, analysing and teasing out their implications before moving on to the next stage of the argument. The case study material varies in source and form – children's work, teacher's work, diary entries, drawings, poetry, literature, interviews. The vitality and richness of primary school practice are conveyed, together with the teacher expertise on which these qualities are based.

Series Editors

Mary Jane Drummond is Tutor in Education, University of Cambridge, Institute of Education, and Andrew Pollard is Professor in the School of Education, University of Bristol.

Series Titles

ASSESSING CHILDREN'S LEARNING
Mary Jane Drummond
1–85346–198–9

COLLABORATIVE LEARNING IN STAFFROOMS AND CLASSROOMS
Colin Biot and Patrick Easen
1–85346–201–2

DEVELOPMENTS IN PRIMARY MATHEMATICS TEACHING
Anne Sawyer
1–85346–196–2

EXPLORING PLAY IN THE PRIMARY CLASSROOM
Gill Beardsley with Penelope Harnett
1–85346–463–5

THE EXPRESSIVE ARTS
Fred Sedgwick
1–85346–200–4

HUMANITIES IN PRIMARY EDUCATION – HISTORY, GEOGRAPHY AND RE IN THE CLASSROOM
Don Kimber, Nick Clough, Martin Forrest, Penelope Harnett, Ian Menter and Elizabeth Newman
1–85346–342–6

IN FAIRNESS TO CHILDREN – WORKING FOR SOCIAL JUSTICE IN THE PRIMARY SCHOOL
Morwenna Griffiths and Carol Davies
1–85346–341–8

LITERACY
Margaret Jackson
1–85346–197–0

ONE CHILD MANY WORLDS – EARLY LEARNING IN MULTICULTURAL COMMUNITIES
Edited by Eve Gregory
1–85346–460–0

PERSONAL, SOCIAL AND MORAL EDUCATION
Fred Sedgwick
1–85346–291–8

PRIMARY DESIGN AND TECHNOLOGY – A PROCESS FOR LEARNING
Ron Ritchie
1–85346–340–X

PRIMARY SCIENCE – MAKING IT WORK, second edition
Chris Ollerenshaw and Ron Ritchie
1–85346–439–2

Introduction

When Penelope Harnett and I first talked about this book we realised we shared a fascination for the ways in which children use imaginative play to explore their ideas about the world. In pretend play and drama activities they often re-enact their experiences, coming to terms with cognitive challenges which they might not otherwise resolve. As teacher educators we were in the privileged position of having visited many classrooms where teachers were incorporating play activities into their planning and using it to further children's understandings of different aspects of the curriculum. At the same time we also had concerns about how these imaginative play experiences could be maintained and valued in the current educational climate.

It would be very easy to extol the virtues of play in the primary classroom and ignore the social and political contexts which influence and shape the actual experiences of children and their teachers. The National Curriculum and its related statutory assessments, OFSTED inspections, action plans and target setting all influence what teachers do in their concern for standards and achievement. In such a context, play is often viewed as recreational by policy makers and parents. This raises important issues for teachers not just about how worthwhile play can be, its value and purpose, but also about how they can justify and explain its inclusion in the primary curriculum.

Alongside the arguments for focusing pupils on the basics, there has always been much interest in play. Seminal work by Bruner, Jolly and Sylva (1977) reflects the rich and diverse observations and research interpreting the different ways in which both children and adults engage in play. A long-established tradition of play as central to learning and development derives from the philosophies of Rousseau, Froebel, Montessori and Isaacs. Their influence in showing the importance of play in pre-school and primary education has been reiterated and examined more recently by Moyles 1988 and 1994, DES 1990a, Anning 1991, Bruce 1991 and Wood and Attfield 1996. It is this background and interest in what play is and what it can offer which makes us want to look again at what is actually taking place when children engage in play.

We have focused on imaginative play because it is an aspect which is easily neglected in the opportunities provided for play in classrooms. Materials may be available for exploratory play as a basis for developing scientific and mathematical concepts or for enhancing design technology. The results of such exploratory play are easily observed, but we sometimes have to look more closely to appreciate children's imaginative ideas in their role play or dramatic activities. Our case studies are examples from busy classrooms. They are not perfect in every way but they do illustrate the many possibilities for developing children's inner worlds through their play. We want to highlight ways of looking and reflecting on children's use of imaginative play in order to justify its place in the planning of their learning experiences.

In the first chapter we ask the question, what is so special about play? How might it be explained to show its importance as an element in children's learning? The model we develop to explore play is based upon a social constructivist approach which draws upon culture, context and interactions.

Chapter 2 examines how play has emerged as a valuable aspect of classroom pedagogy and what this means for teachers. It considers ideas of structure and free play and how these have implications for the primary curriculum. The chapter ends with a number of examples of role-play areas developed in primary classrooms.

Chapter 3 looks more closely at what children think about play and how they view their activities both in and out of the classroom. We look at ways in which teachers may assess what is occurring when children play and how they may help children to reflect on what they do.

Chapter 4 shows how the scripts which emerge in children's imaginative play are an important aspect of their learning and support for one another. We look at opportunities for children to develop their play through texts and themes which promote their imaginative ideas.

In Chapter 5, we look at play and learning in relation to literacy and numeracy and how these areas emerge and are extended within the play process.

In Chapter 6, Penelope Harnett explores how children's understandings of the past can be enriched through play in history and the importance of teachers' own subject knowledge in promoting play activities.

Chapter 7 explores how children construct their social and imaginary worlds through play, examining how play moves into drama and the different ways in which children develop their own plays and narratives.

In conclusion, we look at the politics of play and suggest ways in which teachers might use its many strengths in their planning and assessments of children's progress. In arguing for imaginative role play as part of the curriculum for children throughout the primary age range we appreciate the demands on teachers' time and the concerns they already have in maintaining balance in the curriculum. The introduction of the Literacy Hour for all schools in September 1998, closely followed by equally prescribed time for mathematics, means that we have to be very clear about what play can offer and how it may be incorporated into the activities which contribute to children's learning.

Throughout the book we emphasise our main theme that play is a key process in children's learning throughout their primary schooling and indeed throughout their lives. Play is not seen as additional but as central to learning. As Fisher (1996) has pointed out, it is not something added on or extra. It is with this in mind that we make our exploration of children's play.

CHAPTER 1

What is so Special About Play?

The main focus of this chapter is to argue for the inclusion of imaginative play within the primary curriculum. We begin by examining an episode of play in order to appreciate the processes involved. The chapter goes on to develop a model for under-standing what is taking place when children play and the place of imaginative experiences in helping children to make sense of their worlds. Finally we identify some of the terms in use to describe imaginative play.

Play as a process

Children themselves have always made space for playing. At home, in the street, in playgrounds and many other settings, chil-dren can be seen behaving in ways which suggest that they have their own imaginative agendas. They appear to be imitating things around them, demonstrating the rituals of their everyday lives and pretending they have mastery of the activities they are playing out.

How any episode of play is defined has been based on insights from studies of play in its evolutionary context. Drawing upon Bateson's (1955) evidence of the range of phenomena termed play found in anthropological studies, observers agree that play is tak-ing place because of the signals, messages, negotiations and body language which individuals use to establish that they are playing (Sutton Smith and Kelly Bryne 1984). There are sufficient clues from children's actions and vocalisations, and from the physical settings they may be in, to see the distinction between children's play and other conscious behaviours. The following case study shows the way in which one child demonstrates that she is playing and goes beyond her practical activity into a more imaginative world.

CASE STUDY

The sandpit

Helen and Lesley, both aged four, are playing in a sandpit in an outside play area. This is one of the activities that are always available in their busy nursery. Helen is making pies and spilling and moving the sand. She has collected bricks, a spade and containers. She also moves a small oven to the edge of the sandpit. Helen's actions signal that she is engaged in playing at making sand pies, but she is also influenced by Lesley, who introduces a further imaginative element to the episode.

Figure 1.1 Making pies in the sand

Helen: French pies, loads and loads of French pies. There!
Lesley: They were burning weren't they Mum?
Helen: Yes. Leave it little girl. It hurts my back. Yes, that's how you make it. I stir it round. You put some sugar in. Leave it off – sugar – be careful you do not lose any.
             You are not very young are you?
             Thank you my darling.
             Sugar lumps whole. I put some more sugar lumps in here OK?
             It's a pain with the kids really – she brings sand indoors.
             This hurts my back *(filling bowls).*

Lesley: Mum, can we go round the shops?
Helen: Mind you don't get lost. If you get lost call me.
            Oh no *(sand tips over on the cooker).*
            Go and get over there. Sugar lumps.
            (To Lesley) No love, no more.
            No, in the house over there. She never listens to me.

Throughout the 20 minutes she is playing in the sand Helen is engrossed in her activity. To an onlooker she appears to be experimenting with different kinds of containers to produce her pies. This is what Piaget (1962) refers to as 'representation' or 'memory in action' and is very much at the level of the assimilation of experiential knowledge. She is also showing good coordination with her small spade and the buckets and is very concentrated on her activity. But there is much more going on in Helen's spoken language, often said very quietly and to herself. It is actually Lesley who initiates joint role play and establishes Helen as the mother. Given this cue, Helen uses her imagination to develop her role, drawing on many of the phrases she has heard from her own mother. She develops the parent role through comments such as 'It's a pain with the kids really – she brings sand indoors' as if she is talking to another adult. Helen's observations help her to try out comments she has heard and use them in the context of her own play.

So what is being demonstrated in this short episode and why is it important for Helen? Her motive is to make 'French pies', and the sand is an appropriate medium to do it. Once into role play though, she uses her imagination to create the appropriate language for talking to her daughter and also providing a commentary on her actions. She draws on her memory to use the appropriate language for this role, and for the cooking and interacting with another adult. A number of affective aspects also emerge, such as the 'This hurts my back' and the difficulties with children always making a mess. Vygotsky (1978) terms this type of play 'play with rules'; the rules of the parent–child relationship determining the nature of the language and the play. For example, when Helen role plays a mother she is incorporating the things her own mother might say and do. Vygotsky points out that any form of imaginary play already contains the rules of behaviour. As a mother, Helen follows the rules of maternal behaviour as she has experienced them, so that even though she is free from reality, she is also limited by the framework which Lesley has established for her.

This brief analysis leads us to offer an explanation of imaginative play as a context in which children can bring together their cognitive, social and cultural understandings. Our focus is on play as an imaginative as well as a social construct. Indeed, imagination is, as Vygotsky (1978) points out, central to what occurs when children play. Vygotsky's view is that imaginary situations are the defining characteristics of play and arise from the actions and explorations of themes. He describes play as 'a novel form of behaviour in which the child is liberated from situational constraints through his activity in an imaginary situation' (p. 96).

This emphasis on the imagination suggests the importance of children creating their own versions of their experiences and going beyond them to try out how they think something might be. Vygotsky's view of imaginative play forms the basis for our explanations and in understanding these more fully, and we now turn to notions of play in its wider context.

A social constructivist perspective

The ideas that we develop in this book are based on a social constructivist theory of learning arising from the work of Piaget (1962), Vygotsky (1978) and Bruner (1996) and developed by Donaldson (1983), Haste (1987), Edwards and Mercer (1987), Wood (1988) and Pollard (1993). Although all were writing at different times, taken together their work provides us with a perspective which encompasses the social, cognitive, cultural and affective elements of children's development. Here children are seen as actively involved in the construction of their own knowledge. They develop their learning through interactions with situations and people and through exploration and communication.

Haste (1987, p. 175) provides an account of the different domains which contribute to learning from the social constructivist viewpoint.

She specifies the:

- *intra-individual* domain in which children bring their own level of cognitive complexity to the encounter, assimilate experiences and construct understandings;
- *inter-personal*, or the domain of social interaction, where meanings are negotiated and where the cultural norms and social conventions are learned;
- *socio-historical* domain which draws on the wider context in which learning takes place and is defined by social and cultural practice. It also provides a resource for the rules of interaction as well as for how these rules and orders are interpreted.

We would argue that in episodes of play there are many opportunities for these domains to be brought together (see Helen and Lesley).

Intra-individual	Inter-personal	Socio-historical
Memory in action as Helen plays with sand and containers. She brings her level of complexity to the encounter through reflecting, consolidating and constructing. Her role play is related to experiential knowledge.	Participation in social interaction. Negotiation of meanings with Lesley. Awareness of her role in social interaction.	Culturally defined expectations in her language use related to behaviour between family members.

Figure 1.2 Play in different domains

Play can provide opportunities for children to play at their own level of complexity, interact and learn to negotiate with others and draw upon the social and cultural practices which are part of their lives. The map shown in Figure 1.3 is a way of describing how this might occur.

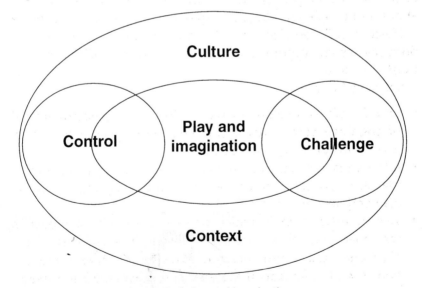

Figure 1.3 Interactive features of play and imagination

The starting point for explaining this map is the opportunities play can provide for children to develop their imagination.

Play and imagination

In looking at the notion of play as a means of enabling children to make more sense of their lives, we wish to emphasise imagination and the emotions often related to it. Weininger (1988) conceptualises imagination as the 'thinking function' of pretend play or 'thinking through what one might do in a particular role or situation' (p. 144). In other words, when children are in a play context or have identified a theme, the way in which they interpret their theme or role requires a 'what if' question to take the ideas further. Often this occurs as children are bringing items together or playing with different objects. Their talk is almost for themselves as they move between their real and imaginative worlds in establishing the form of their play.

In the following example we see what happens when children are able to follow their own lines of thinking during an episode of free play. It shows the way their imagination can take off at different points, opening up new possibilities which enable children to flow in and out of the play according to their own needs and concerns.

CASE STUDY

Lego models

Trevor and Peter, both aged five, have got the Lego box and set out the pieces on the carpet.

Trevor: I'll go and get a little bit first. Those bits first. Look Peter like that, then that.

Peter: Zoom my space ship here it comes.

Trevor: That how you do it Peter, is that how it goes?

Peter: Good. You put it in there.

Trevor: Then you put the two on the top.

Peter: No you can't. It isn't finished yet.

Trevor: Peter, I am going to get a little animal – an elephant in a big house. *(He pulls a box of animals towards him.)*
I see a mouse on Tom and Jerry.
Yours can be a spider house.

Peter: No, I want my own. No Trevor, it looks funny. If we have it as a boat it can be a boat.

Trevor: I'll have the spider first. Why don't I put him in the little drawer? *(The drawer in his model.)*

Peter: Why?

Trevor: Pull it along right – this is for rescue right. Put the chicken down there. That can be yours and that can be mine. *(He takes the spider round flying like a plane for a while.)*

Initially the children are collaborating with one another in making the same model, but it soon becomes apparent that they each see it differently and want it to be different things. Peter then begins to develop his own model which Trevor tries to add to by bringing in small animals. This leads to a protest from Peter: 'No Trevor, it looks funny.'

Each child's imagination and feelings are an essential part of their play. Trevor is wanting approval and using imagination to make the model into different things as they add pieces to it. But he pushes Peter too far and Peter strongly protests, asserting his idea about the boat. Both boys are using the 'what if' function as they add things to the model. Peter begins with a spaceship and then goes on to a boat. His 'If we have it as a boat it can be a boat' is most revealing in showing that in play you imagine something to be something else as you wish. Trevor brings in a further imaginative idea with the 'elephant' and the 'spider house'.

As they express their feelings they are also thinking about the kind of model they wish to make. Peter's 'No you can't. It isn't finished yet' and 'No, I want my own. No Trevor, it looks funny' reveals his feelings of irritation which are related to his thinking about how he wants the model to be. Initially, Peter shows empathy and appreciates Trevor's need for approval in adding pieces to the model when he says 'Good. You put it in there.' We have here what Egan (1988, p. 121) describes as our 'unique isolated consciousness' which is never the same as others, but enables us to reach out and appreciate other people's personal meanings. Thus imagination is a power which is not only intellectual but emerges as much from children's emotions as from their thinking (Egan 1988).

This episode is included to show that often when children are engaged in their free play in the classroom much more is happening than we may think. Both children in the example move in and out of their real and pretend worlds as their play develops and each tries to create his own fantasy episode. Frequently teachers do not have the time to observe what is taking place in play settings and may need to use some of the strategies suggested in Chapter 3. Nevertheless, we should not underestimate the interactions and emotional understandings which may be taking place.

Moving to other aspects of the play map we see how episodes of play emerge within specific contexts and the overall culture from which they derive.

Culture and context

If we consider the context in which episodes of play are embedded we can see that cultural practices provide the framework and the patterns which children use to construct their own versions of their experiences and their understandings of the world. Bruner stresses that 'It is culture that provides the tools for organising and understanding our worlds in communicable ways' (1996, p. 3).

Play reflects the world of popular culture and enables children to use and make sense of it. The toys, videos, books and artefacts available for any age group reflect the media world in which children live and the concerns which are a part of their lives and those of their families and friends. It is this cultural background which often emerges in play as children flow in and out of imaginary situations and reality. Indeed they often use elements of their culture to embellish their interpretations of events in their play.

Two nine-year-olds are playing with a playmobile fort. They have spent a great deal of time planning the action, based on the Norman Conquest. They are using miniature people as soldiers and it is with great exuberance that the following conversation takes place.

Harry: I have got some important news. We have just had a fax from the Normans. It said that they are going to come and ask William the Conqueror to be King.

Tim: He conquered a bit of land behind our back garden. He could probably conquer us.

Harry: Let us set a trap unless he comes along in his Formula 1 racing car. The fax said he was coming today.

These boys easily move from past to present in their use of language and enjoy the joke of playing with possibilities from their present culture. Being able to bring these ideas together occurs naturally as part of their play. Their individual knowledge of language enables them to create their own versions and define new forms of behaviour. Thus, when children use language in unusual ways in their play they are creating their own version of an event. The unconscious nature of this learning results from making certain intuitive responses within the rule-governed behaviour of which it is a part. Children are therefore in this 'culture-producing framework' in which, by taking part in social activity that amends rules or generates new ones, they are able to produce their own cultural forms. As we saw above, it is a very active and creative participation on the part of children. Bruner probably explains these cultural interpretations best when he says: 'Although meanings are "in the mind" they have their origin and their significance in the culture in which they are created. It is this cultural situatedness of meanings that assures their negotiability and ultimately their communicability.' (1996, p. 41)

The contexts in which play episodes occur also determine the play which takes place and the rules of that play. The children playing with the soldiers knew that the use of technology and present-day objects would be funny in the context of the soldier's game. They were able to use that context to create the joke.

In schools children learn the culture through hearing about it from siblings and their peer group and observing routines and events and hearing the language around them. They have certain expectations about how to behave in different classroom situations. The process of learning how to listen to stories in a nursery is clearly demonstrated by Betty Cochran Smith (1984) in *The Making of a Reader*. In her story-reading sessions, her nursery children learned to be literate through a process of socialisation rather than by direct teaching. They discovered the meanings of emphasis on vocabulary, intonations and actions in the cultural contexts of the school. These occurred through interactions such as:

- readiness interactions which established or maintained the physical and psychological story reading frame. Coming to sit on the carpet established the story reading context;
- life-to-text interactions which helped children to draw on their own experiences to make sense of the texts;
- text-to-life interactions which helped children to make sense of their own experiences.

In these story sessions children learned about the culture of hearing a story, the expectations and what it implied; all part of 'learning school'.

Children's learning in a subject such as PE also depends upon particular rules which determine how they should behave. Children have expectations of these rules and become concerned if they are not maintained. Similarly, play in the school context will often be focused according to the themes the class may be engaged in or as a result of the physical opportunities of space and equipment. It will be determined by the fact that it is in the classroom and therefore is a certain kind of play which children will interpret accordingly. This is not to suggest that play in the classroom is not worthwhile, but that we are talking about a structured form of play in which the boundaries are clearly defined by the physical setting and the definitions which often emerge through the curriculum.

Turning to other aspects of the play map, there are opportunities for both control and challenge to occur for children within their play. In the following example, a Year 2 class are invited to play in Sunshine City. They have created this play area in their school hall using cardboard boxes and other materials.

The children and their teachers had made shops, a cafe, a Victorian music hall, houses, streets, a church and a hospital as well as adding cars, buses, prams, furniture and dressing-up clothes. They had also made notices for all the different areas and added print as required, such as a rota for the cafe. The children could be seen engrossed in mending lorries, dressing up, being customers and shopkeepers. There was little adult intervention or expectation other than asking the children to think about what they might do before they moved into the area.

What began to emerge in the play in Sunshine City was the involvement of all children in their activities. Having planned and put together the different elements, they were free to use it in imaginative ways and decide what they wished to do and how. As we observed the play taking place there were many occasions when children were concentrated in the 'flow' of their play (Csikszentmihalyi 1979). This implies total involvement and a lack of self-consciousness through absorption in the activity. There were also opportunities for children to be in control and challenged through their activities.

Control

One of the characteristics of play in general is the space it creates for children to be in control of their activities and to move in and out of a play episode as they wish. In the following examples we focus on how children control what they do as they become immersed in their imaginative roles.

CASE STUDY

Sunshine City

In the garage in Sunshine City, two boys mending a lorry were engaged in very specific detail as they used screwdrivers, chisels and drills to change a wheel or drill into the metal. They had an Owners' Workshop Manual open in front of them and referred to it often.

Daniel: Can I borrow the drill a minute?
Joshua: Right Daniel, I'll tell you when to put it in.
Daniel: OK.
Joshua: I'll tell you when to stop.
Don't stop.
Stop.

All of this was carried out with appropriate actions showing exactly what these children had learned from watching mechanics at work. They were also completely in control of their activity and engrossed in it. While this example is not unusual when we observe children playing, it is interesting to see what occurs when children have the space to follow their own interests. In setting up the context of Sunshine City there had been many discussions with the children about the kinds of notices that might be around and where items were placed. In the corner of the hall was a 'Mr & Mrs Fix It' sign where children returned with their tools and where they used Lego and Duplo, and dismantled old video editing machines and record players. There was much intense activity and exploration as the children discovered how they could take things apart and create things as they wished.

In another area of Sunshine City there was a 'Sparkles' jewellers with many items which had been made by the children. A list of prices had been decided, together with instructions on how to write cheques or use credit cards. The following discussion occurred between two customers and the shopkeeper:

Customer 1: How much is this?
Customer 2: Look at the ticket.
Shopkeeper: Alright you have enough. 50p off then. *(Puts item in green bag.)* There you are.
Customer 1: Can I have a necklace and a watch?
Shopkeeper: This is the cheapest of all the watches, 10p.

Referring back to our map, we can see that these children were drawing on their culture by showing their knowledge of the social context of a jeweller's shop. They were also imagining what it would be like to be the shopkeeper or a customer. Those who took on the roles were in control of events and were able to meet the challenge of what this meant. They also had opportunities to try out their knowledge of using money. The processes of buying and selling, discounts and comparisons of prices are all demonstrated in this short example, showing one way in which children's understandings can emerge as part of the flow of their play.

Vygotsky's (1978) notion of play creating 'zones of proximal development' provides an explanation of how, in their play, children may try out activities and skills they have not yet achieved. They may also demonstrate knowledge which is not yet fully understood. Children try out in their play the actions and rules of what they would like to be able to do before they can do it, for example driving a bus, writing menus and being a mechanic. A zone of proximal development is best defined as 'the distance between the actual developmental level as determined by independent problem solving and the level of potential development as determined through problem solving under adult guidance or in collaboration with more capable peers' (Vygotsky 1978, p. 86).

In the context of Sunshine City there were several examples of children pretending to solve a problem which could only actually be achieved with the help of a more capable other or an adult. Several children, for example, were using Roamers and making them move along streets chalked out on the floor. They helped one another to turn the models around and move them in different directions. One boy, Sam, was having some difficulties; the teacher intervened and helped him to program the machine. Once he had been successful a couple of times she left him to continue on his own. Sam soon joined the other children.

Sam: Forward 1. I am the police. I will make this car go to the police station now.

Identifying Sam's zone of proximal development was important in enabling him to move forward in his learning and also to take on the imaginative aspect of his play. As a teacher it is not always easy to pick up on a child's particular developmental level, but being able to observe activities in this kind of context can give opportunities to see where specific teaching might be focused.

It would seem that play is part of a continuum in which there is a merging of action and awareness. It provides a way for children to control how their activities develop. When children behave in a way which suggests they are performing an act of play which represents something they may have experienced, we can call this 'play for real'. Such activity may include considerable effort and emotional tension as aspects of their understandings are demonstrated. What is clear is that the centring of attention upon a self-chosen task in which one can be in control is an important element in gaining skills.

Challenge

Piaget's (1962) view that 'playfulness' signifies knowledge that is so well assimilated that it can be played with, suggests that this is usually accompanied by feelings of confidence. The events leading up to this, however, are often of a different nature and could give rise to situations in which children are in cognitive confusion or conflict. Athey's (1990) research, which documented 20 young children's developmental behaviour over a two-year period from the age of two to four, showed examples of events leading to knowledge being assimilated. Over 80 per cent of the children's affective responses showed surprise, struggle or perturbation. The researchers felt that the stimulating environment of the project, in which children were brought once a week by their parents to a centre to participate in 'play' activities, may have generated challenge and struggle. In the activities the 'play' element gave rise to cognitive conflict as well as enjoyment before mastery was achieved.

This research emphasises the seriousness with which children engage in play and the time needed to 'accommodate' and explore new materials or situations before a more imaginative phase can occur. It would seem that this is not something which happens sequentially. Children appear to move in and out of situations which might be challenging. This frequently happens in imaginative play where, as long as the play is loose enough, an individual child can make some aspect of the experience particularly significant.

A group of children in Sunshine City were playing with plastic blocks and using them to make a post office. Some of the blocks become parcels, others chairs and tables. They drew on their understanding of how a post office works, their early writing and their ability to represent different objects with the blocks. One child collected paper and pens from the classroom and was recording the parcels:

David: Yes, but he's got to write them down.
John: All the parcels?
David: No, but this one hasn't been wrote down yet has it Jason?

Here the writing was the element of the play that David wished to make important. He was able to use the play context to try out his mark making and experiment with what he knew about writing. He was playing with what he was also learning to do in other classroom contexts. The play provided him with opportunities to practice and try out his writing in his own way.

The ideas we have been discussing so far suggest that play is a challenge which enables children to meet objects and situations that are new to them. Explorations with new materials or situations may create struggle and uncertainty until the possibilities are fully understood. Nevertheless, play is also an activity that can be innovative, original, creative and imaginative, as we have tried to show in these different settings.

Defining our terms

There are a number of terms to describe the kinds of play activities we refer to throughout this book. 'Pretend play', 'role play', 'fantasy play', 'imaginative play', 'free-flow play', 'dramatic play' and 'sociodramatic play' are all terms in use and are often interchangeable without being clearly defined. Drawing upon the work of Piaget (1962), Singer and Singer (1990), Smilanski (1990), Bruce (1991) and Booth (1994) we show in the box opposite some of the characteristics of these descriptions of children's play activities.

Imagination and *fantasy* are important in all the categories described. The notion of exploratory play leading to imaginative play is useful here. Children may experiment with objects and ideas before they use them in imaginative ways. Finding out a home play area has baby dolls and a baby bath enables a child to imagine being a mother or father and bathing the baby. It also brings in the emotional aspects of imagining being in another role. The term 'free-flow play' has been used by Goncu (1987) to describe imaginative, free and creative play, and this has been explored in detail by Bruce (1991; see next chapter).

Smilanski (1990) stresses the complexities in sociodramatic play of the integrating and planning, organisation, reasoning, representation and the social skills involved in the activities.

Pretend play:
- imitation with an object or number of objects;
- sometimes in a sequence;
- imitation of actions;
- make believe, drawing from experiential knowledge of objects, roles and situations;
- acting out 'what if' situations, for example 'What if I am the doctor and you break your leg?'

Role play:
- where a role is taken on through imitation, orally or in verbal interactions. Part of this process includes building up relationships with other people.

Dramatic play:
- more of an overall term which includes pretend and role play;
- draws on the imagination using first- and second-hand experiences to develop elements of the play;
- includes the use of props and is dependent upon language.

Sociodramatic play:
- here dramatic play would include two or more players;
- interaction and collaboration within the framework of an episode;
- ongoing improvisations as children make something of their roles as the play develops.

In addition there is the flexibility and spontaneity which occurs in children's choice of roles and how these develop within an episode. Smilanski points out that in a school context participation in identified themes brings in elements of sociodramatic play and drama. She states:

Playing a role demands enough intellectual discipline to include only behaviour appropriate for the role which is being taken on.

In order to act within a sociodramatic episode, the child must grasp the essence of things – the major features of a character or theme, the central characteristics.

Participation teaches the child to concentrate on a specific theme.

Participation requires children to control themselves, to discipline their own actions with regard to episodic content, themes and roles they have taken on.

Different approaches to the story line encourage flexibility.

Children learn new approaches to concepts and dilemmas.

They learn to move forward from representation through to abstract thought.

The more children engage in sociodramatic play the more they develop varied interpretations of roles and situations.

(Adapted from Smilanski 1990, pp. 25–6.)

Although Smilanski is referring to sociodramatic play, the move into drama is a subtle one as children become more disciplined in their interpretations of roles and episodes within an overall structure.

Drama:
- provides a more stylised form of play which includes techniques and improvisations as children take on particular roles and representations;
- may include some kind of public performance within the class or school.

A useful distinction of the play mode moving into drama is given by Booth (1994), who says: 'There will of course be times when children will engage in drama in a spontaneous and open ended structure, maintaining the "as if" situation and developing the action without intervention by the teacher. They will be working in a play mode ...' (p. 27).

Booth also points out that for teachers of drama 'It is a continual process of organization and reorganization, of focusing and refocusing. I must try to see the implications of every suggestion and then find an appropriate strategy for utilising the ideas for the larger overall educational goals of the group.' (1994, p. 13)

A sophisticated version of the play mode leading to drama is apparent when junior-aged children are planning for a dramatic production. A group of ten- and eleven-year-old children were preparing a play based on the journeys of John Cabot. They were doing this in their after-school drama club and were involved in all aspects of the production. They had to organise the sequence of the play and different episodes in each act; they had to write their parts and develop them within the theme of the story. A considerable amount of discussion, collaboration and negotiation occurred in order to get their different ideas represented. In the course of the acting there was spontaneity and ongoing improvisation as they responded to one another within each episode. As the rehearsals went on the children appreciated the need to have a set text and finalised this as a basis for the production. Although this was a formal representation of a play, the children had freedom to control and change their activities within the overall pattern it. They made all the decisions about changes and mimes and so on, which meant that the play was not only a challenge, but all their own. For these children their play mode became drama as they took on the features of the dramatic production.

Summary

In this chapter we have tried to show that opportunities for pretend or imaginative play enable children of all ages to make representations which symbolise aspects of their cultural and social worlds. In many primary classrooms, play has been recognised and accepted as important in providing concrete experiences leading to mental operations, or as a vehicle for personal and social development. We would argue that we need to look closely at what extra opportunities imaginative role play might offer for enabling children to appreciate and make more sense of their emotional lives.

Vygotsky's notion that play is part of children's development and that it is imaginative play which defines the activity as play for them, suggests that in moving into play children have incentives to act in certain ways and play out unrealised thoughts or actions they do not yet understand. In providing contexts for imaginative play we are giving children opportunities to rehearse and create their own versions of their social and emotional experiences. By observing these interpretations of children's different worlds, teachers are provided with further information about their understanding and learning.

CHAPTER 2

Play in Classrooms: Contexts and Opportunities

This chapter shows how play as a form of expression became recognised as characteristic child behaviour. We consider the work of early educationalists to show how play came to be given educational value and was seen as important in contributing to emotional development. The second part of the chapter examines the difference between structured and free play and what this means for the kinds of play opportunities teachers can provide in the classroom. The chapter ends with examples of how play themes can be developed for different ages in the primary school.

Traditions of play

We begin by examining the sets of ideas which have informed our views of play; how it came to be seen as valuable both in terms of mental processes and in children's imaginary lives. It is interesting to note that the concept of freedom for imaginative play to develop is not as evident as one might think. Play in educational settings has always been viewed as a means of encouraging exploration and learning and structured accordingly.

By the beginning of the nineteenth century, the idea of childhood not just being a preparation for adult life but existing in its own right as a special period of life was gradually gaining acceptance. Pestalozzi, Froebel and Montessori developed and put into practice their ideas for a suitable learning environment for young children.

The ideas of Pestalozzi (1746–1827) were influential in the work of Robert Owen when he set up the first infant school in Scotland (1816; see Whitbread 1972), which included opportunities for children to engage in free outdoor play. In England the infant school movement spread through the work and writings of Samuel Wilderspin who provided a model for the kind of activities appropriate for young children in his *On the Importance of Educating the Infant Children of the Poor* (1823; see Whitbread 1972). He believed in adapting instruction to the capacities of young children and this included practical activities in arithmetic, time spent in outside play with appropriate equipment and the verbal repetition of instructional rhymes and rules. Even then it was acknowledged that young children needed to have materials which enabled them to be active as well as learning by rote.

Although somewhat idealistic, Froebel (1782–1852) was among the first to suggest the significance of educative play in young children's development (Froebel 1826). He saw it as crucial in helping them to absorb knowledge and for their imagination, creativity and language. He stressed play as an integrating mechanism in which children could demonstrate their learning experiences and use the knowledge they had processed and transformed. The active involvement of children with the arts, natural sciences, written and spoken language and physical activity were all critical parts of his approach to learning.

Froebel tried to devise a pedagogy which was essentially child centred and where the teacher was a passive follower rather than an instructor. It was his ideas and strong belief in the importance of play which provided a basis for the notion of 'active learning'. When the first Froebelian kindergarten was opened in Hampstead, England (by Madam Ronge, who had worked in a Froebel kindergarten in Germany), the idea of 'active learning' was stressed. This occurred through exploration with highly structured educational material called 'gifts, of increasing complexity'. For example, the third 'gift' was a box containing a two-inch cube, divided once in every direction and forming eight small cubes of one inch each for children to play with and put together in a variety of designated forms. An example of an occupation was paper weaving, where coloured paper in the form of strips and bases for interweaving was provided. These activities reflected the exploratory and active nature of the learning that was being encouraged through 'playing' with particular materials.

Montessori (1870–1952) argued that during their first seven years children needed to be separated from the world, in order to learn in a planned environment. The inner lives of children were encouraged through prepared and graded sequences of activities which enabled them to absorb and appreciate aspects of their environment through their senses. Concentration on the way flowers may look or smell, for example, encouraged children to express their feelings, but in a structured way. The finely graded wooden apparatus used to further perception and mathematical concepts was part of an approach through the senses which was calm and controlled. Children were given freedom to move about, even though within strictly defined limits. It was an approach which eventually contributed to infant schools encouraging exploration through sensory experiences.

In this country, Susan Isaacs (1885–1948) perhaps more than any other educationalist, did much to promote the importance of play and exploration and to examine this from the viewpoint of developmental psychology. In her work at the Maltings School in Cambridge and at the Department of Child Development at the University of London Institute of Education, she approached the function of nursery education from her scientific study of psychology and from systematic child observation. The advertisement she answered to work at the Maltings School asked for 'a university graduate – or someone of equivalent intellectual standing who has hitherto considered themselves too good for teaching and who has probably already engaged in another occupation' (Gardner 1969, pp. 54–5).

Although this was a somewhat unusual and challenging opportunity, Isaacs had the appropriate knowledge from her psychological and philosophical studies and was able to put into practice the most advanced educational thought of the time drawn from philosophy, psychology and logic, as well as building on new ideas which were emerging from psychoanalysis and the writings of Freud.

One of Isaacs' main aims was to encourage clear thinking and independent behaviour. She concentrated on the child's need to find out and the influence of language on thought and emotions. Her work was of the greatest importance in its contribution to our understanding of the intellectual and social development of young children and the reality of problem solving and thinking through play. Although influenced by Froebel, Piaget (who visited the school) and Dewey, she was a pioneer for new ways of looking at child development and progress. In her biography of Susan Isaacs, Gardner (1969) noted how often Isaacs stressed the importance of observation and 'how important it is in all studies to take account of how much more children can reveal to us in all aspects of their development if we observe them objectively in situations of their everyday life' (1969, p. 161).

In all Susan Isaacs' work she stressed the intellectual challenge in encouraging children to be active in their learning and to explore their environment. This involved the teacher being positive in promoting learning by providing support and intervention where it was needed. The writings of Susan Isaacs encouraged many educationalists to appreciate the value of play and to see it as an essential part of children's experiences in the development of their thinking.

The Hadow Reports of 1931 and 1933 (see Board of Education 1931, 1933) helped to clarify and summarise the development of the first 60 years of compulsory schooling. They also set the scene for what was to follow. Hadow reflected marked changes in official opinion in establishing the characteristics of the modern 'primary school'. Although they did not actually mention play, above all the reports introduced enjoyment into the education of young children: 'The curriculum of the Primary School must be thought of in terms of activity and experience rather than knowledge to be acquired and facts to be stored' (Board of Education 1931, p. 139). While Hadow also had much to say about methodology, it was some time before the pedagogy of primary education began to reflect these ideas.

Play was perhaps given its strongest endorsement to date as part of the pedagogues of primary education in the Plowden Report (Central Advisory Council for Education 1967). Child centredness and learning through activity were particularly strong messages and were encouraged through providing opportunities for children's play. The report emphasised the importance of play in nursery and infant education by presenting it as a feature of the child-centred approach it advocated: 'Young children learn best through an informal setting and play is important in their development ... Wide ranging and satisfying play is a means of learning ...' (Plowden 1967, p. 194).

Critics of the Plowden ideology saw it as too permissive and interpreted it as allowing too much freedom with too little direction (Dearden 1968). How far the child-centred interpretation was actually adopted in the traditional climates of primary classrooms is difficult to judge. However, although the idea of providing a stimulating environment in which active learning could occur did emerge as an important aspect of primary pedagogy, the movement against progressive education was gathering speed. In the 1970s Cox and Boyson (1975, 1979) and Bennett (1976) echoed the concern for standards and contributed to parental unease about so-called progressive methods in education.

Twenty years on there has been much more of an emphasis on exploration and learning within the framework of a constant concern for maintaining standards, particularly in the basic skills. The value of sand or water play has been acknowledged in nursery and infant schools as the beginnings of understanding mathematical and scientific concepts. But the actual terminology has changed in order to give more of a purposeful sound to the activity. 'Active learning' is now frequently used in primary schools to refer to experiential approaches where children have the freedom to explore objects or materials.

The term also reflects an approach which encourages investigation and experimentation. We do not always acknowledge that many classroom activities provide opportunities for children to 'play' with new ideas, concepts and equipment. Using CD-ROMs, exploring different art techniques, and looking at exploded photographs in information books all enable children to play with what they know and explore and extend their own knowledge with their peers.

So far we have shown how thinking about the value of play has been closely associated with children's cognitive understandings. We now look at ways in which the emotional side of children's lives emerges through their imaginative play.

Play as part of children's imaginative lives

Frequently the seriousness and intensity of children's play indicate its importance to them. Froebel stated that 'Play is the highest level of child development. It is the spontaneous expression of thought and feeling – an expression which his inner life requires. This is the meaning of the word "play".' (1887, p. 43)

For Froebel then, play was not only valuable in educational terms but a requirement for a healthy inner life; he stressed the free choice of play in enabling children to reveal their minds, understandings and emotions.

Both Froebel and later Caldwell Cook (1917) appreciated that interest and involvement were crucial elements in play and that play was a way of integrating and unifying children's learning. Cook was one of the earliest educators to argue that play was closely associated with the concept of work. He stated that 'When work and play are separated, the one becomes mere drudgery, the other a mere pastime. Neither is then of any value in life. It is the core of my faith that the only work worth doing is really play; for by play I mean the doing anything with one's heart in it.' (1917, p. 4)

Cook based his book *The Play Way* on his daily evidence from his own practice of children's capacity to explore experiences through the imagination. He argued that make-believe play enabled them to be in control of their activities and also to experiment and rehearse aspects of their lives. He claimed: 'It is possible to hold rehearsals, to try our strength in a make-believe big world. And that is play.' (1917, p. 6)

Make-believe play was also seen as important for emotional development. In her psychoanalytic studies of emotionally disturbed children, Melanie Klein, who began her work in 1919, stressed the importance of spontaneous play as a substitute for the verbal association approach Freud had employed with adults. Her use of miniature toys for projective play assumed that what children did in free play symbolised their wishes, fears, pleasures and conflicts and the preoccupations they might not be aware of. Her series of case studies was particularly influential in showing the value of play in children's lives. She stressed that children revealed their feelings in free play, the role of the adult being to reassure them of the meaningfulness of their play activities. The role of the therapist was to help to interpret their play for them. Initially Klein's ideas were quite revolutionary as they diverged from Freudian methods of analysis. As her work became well known she influenced later ideas about the educational value of play and its importance in modifying children's behaviour. Play began to be accepted as the child's way of exploring and coming to terms with the world.

Lowenfeld's book *Play in Childhood* (1935) also recorded the ways in which children were able to reflect their intensely emotional responses through play. In a number of extensive case studies, she showed the importance of play as an essential part of a healthy life. Children often role play their emotional experiences so that they can feel more in control of what is taking place and can come to terms with their feelings in safety. Lowenfeld concluded that normal and satisfactory emotional development was not possible without opportunities for such expression.

Although approaching play from different viewpoints, Froebel, Caldwell Cook, Klein and Lowenfeld all acknowledged play, and particularly imaginative play, as an activity which provides children with opportunities to examine seriously the things they do not fully understand. The imaginative situations children create through their play enable them to try out and extend their knowledge in an alternative world which is outside their real-life situations. These imaginative situations might not only include aspects of their emotional lives, but also the efforts and imagination required for intellectual understanding to occur.

Vygotsky's view that after early childhood children's play 'must always be interpreted as the imaginary, illusory realisation of unrealisable desires' (1966, p. 539) suggests that in considering cognitive aspects of play we should not neglect the affective situation and the circumstances which may influence children's activities.

We now return to play as it is viewed within our current context. In spite of a common belief amongst educationalists that play is central to our present understanding of learning and development, it is rarely given a focus within classroom settings. We now look at what play in classrooms means for teachers and how it is interpreted.

Play in classrooms

As we saw in the first chapter, one of the characteristics of true play is the freedom it provides for children to explore and make sense of their experiences. Tina Bruce (1991) draws on Goncu's (1987) phrase 'free-flow play' to describe imaginative, free and creative play. She identifies 12 features of free-flow play which suggest children being very much in control of the activity.

According to Bruce, the features of free-flow play are:

- it is an active process without a product;
- it is intrinsically motivated;
- it exerts no pressure to conform to rules, pressures, goals, tasks or definite direction;
- it is about possible alternative worlds which involve 'supposing' and 'as if' which lift players to their highest level of functioning. This involves being imaginative, creative, original and innovative;
- it is about participants wallowing in ideas, feelings and relationships;
- it involves reflecting on and becoming aware of what we know or 'metacognition';
- it actively uses previous first hand experiences, including struggle, manipulation, exploration, discovery and practice;
- it is sustained, and when in full flow, helps us to function in advance of what we actually do in our real lives. During free flow play we use the technical prowess, mastery and competence we have previously developed so we can be in control;
- it can be initiated by a child or an adult, but each must be sensitive to each other's personal agenda;
- it can be solitary;
- it can be in partnerships, or groups of adults or children who will be sensitive to each other;
- it is an integrating mechanism, which brings together everything we think, know, feel and understand. (From Bruce 1991, pp. 59–60)

While these features of free-flow play are worthy of consideration and bring together much which has emerged from the ideas of the early educationalists, where do features of free-flow play leave teachers in planning for play and justifying its purpose? Primary teachers represent an amalgam of understandings about teaching and learning which contribute to the approaches, methods and attitudes which they employ at any given time (Pollard *et al.* 1994). These understandings arise through the particular culture of the schools in which they work and of the classroom contexts in which they find themselves.

Bennett, Wood and Rogers' (1997) studies of nine reception class teachers' theories of play show that they see it as important and as part of their thinking and actions when working with young children. The teachers in the study agreed that:

- children's ideas and interests are central to play;
- play provides the ideal conditions in which to learn and enhances the quality of learning;
- a sense of ownership is central to children's learning through play;
- learning is more relevant if it is self-initiated;
- children learn how to learn through play;
- children are more likely to remember what they have done in play;
- learning through play happens easily, without fear and without erecting barriers;
- play is natural – children are themselves;
- play is developmentally appropriate – children know intuitively what they need and meet these needs through play;
- play enables children to explore and experiment;
- children cannot fail in play as there are no rights or wrongs;
- play enables teachers to observe real learning;
- children experience less frustration in play, which reduces discipline problems. (From Bennett *et al.* 1997, p. 32)

While many teachers would echo these ideas and see some play as valuable, it would seem not all play is viewed as useful or purposeful. The teachers in Bennett's study were keen to promote purposeful play which would encourage children's development and learning. They saw play as serving multiple purposes such as:

- exploration and investigation prior to a teacher-directed activity;
- a free, unstructured activity with little adult direction or intervention;
- a context for developing skills and concepts introduced in teacher-directed activities;
- a context for realising defined intentions. (From Bennett *et al.* 1997, pp. 55–6.)

They felt there was a need to provide some kind of structure to the play which was on offer in their classrooms.

Taken altogether, the ideas from the early educators, Bruce and the teachers in Bennett's study provide a powerful argument for the use of play in promoting children's development and learning. We now look at how far teachers are able to fulfil their ideologies about play within the contexts in which they work. We focus particularly on the ways in which structured and purposeful play has been interpreted.

Structure, purpose or just play?

The word 'structure' is frequently associated with classroom learning and implies the opportunities which are provided by teachers to encourage children to work through an activity. 'Structured' and 'unstructured' were terms first used by Manning and Sharp (1977) to refer to play initiated by teachers or play which was child initiated. In her work on block play, Gura (1992) identified three levels of teacher involvement: the *'laissez faire'* approach where children were free to play as they wished; a more *'didactic'* approach where the play was set and dominated by adults; and the *'interactionist'* approach where adults and children were partners in the play. These are useful distinctions and many teachers feel a need to use all three approaches at some time in children's play episodes. Even so, children often create their own rules! Children themselves may structure their play according to their own wishes and it would be a mistake to assume that they do not have an idea of how their play will develop, as we see from the following example in which Mark uses a classroom play setting to develop his own play theme.

Mark has chosen to play in the shop in his reception class. He gets a large black bag and shovels in money from the till, the till itself and various goods on sale. His teacher notices this and asks him what he is doing. Mark replies, 'I'm the robber, I'm robbing the shop'. His teacher explains that if he does this other children will not be able to play there and he rather grudgingly returns everything to its place.

This is not an unusual occurrence and teachers are left with the dilemma of using such an episode as an opportunity for personal and social development or letting children play out their ideas and experiences as they wish.

Neil Kitson (1997) argues strongly for adult intervention in children's sociodramatic and fantasy play. This means adults interacting and playing with children in the particular themes being played out, an idea also supported by Smilanski (1968). Intervention by a teacher or other adults may be valuable and necessary in promoting and developing play activities, particularly if the teacher wishes to extend children's imagination and encourage different lines of thought. In studies of adult intervention in play activities, Smilanski (1968) and Smilanski and Shefatya (1990) found that where teachers or other adults initiated fantasy and role play with small groups of children, the children were helped to sustain and develop it over a period of time.

Smilanski (1968) refers to 'outside' and 'inside' intervention. Outside intervention involves the adult in making comments from outside the situation in order to encourage or further the actions of the participants. Inside intervention involves the adult as part of the play and taking a role within it. Both forms can be enriching in encouraging children to make use of the play materials available. She also found that children often imitated the behaviour of the teacher model and generalised it to fit new situations, but this is not always the case and intervention may restrict children's knowledge and ideas. It would also seem that some interventions from teachers who wish to instruct or promote skills through play can limit the opportunities for children to show the knowledge they already possess.

For us, this raises the question, is it really play when adults intervene? Where adults are interrupting the flow they may well take away from the imaginative ideas which children have.

Joining in needs to be on children's terms and carried out sensitively in order to appreciate what their needs might be; Isaacs' stress on observation should always be the starting point. Nevertheless, even this can go wrong at times, as one of us found out when observing five-year-olds playing with construction toys in a reception classroom:

Trevor: Why don't you come and play with us then?
Observer: Alright, what shall I be?
Trevor: You can hold this piece of crane while Jack and I fix it to work.

We all get put in our places in the end!

We would argue that all play in classrooms is to some extent structured due to the provision and availability of the space, physical layout, equipment and materials. The rules of the situation are clearly set by the context. Many teachers provide a loose structure by supplying materials which indicate a particular theme for the play but leaving children to add to the ideas as they wish and to develop their own play episodes.

Issues such as structure and intervention leave us with questions about how we plan for play in the classroom and what kinds of play we are trying to promote. Where play is incorporated into the themes or topics of the classroom there are many opportunities for children to develop their imaginative play within a loose framework which is provided. Establishing an area where children are able to use their imagination and explore their ideas would seem a valuable element in the learning taking place. A group of teachers who were recently discussing the value of a role-play area identified the following possibilities for children's learning:

- modelling life experiences;
- social development;
- empathy;
- sharing;
- imagination;
- cooperation;
- communication;
- use of technical and specialised vocabulary;

- confidence;
- opportunities for developing curriculum areas such as reading and writing in informal ways.

It is this range of learning opportunities that imaginative play can provide which we would wish to develop.

Opportunities for play

A home area is popular in nurseries and many infant classrooms and provides a valuable link between home and school in enabling children to play out their home experiences in familiar settings. Many teachers like to retain home-area play because of these links and research has shown that the home area is often the most popular play activity in pre-school settings (Pellegrini 1984). However, the home area can also be one of the most under-resourced, culturally biased and unimaginative areas in class-rooms and it is important that children have opportunities to use appropriate and up-to-date materials which are of good quality and realistic to handle (see Figure 2.1).

Nor should we forget the value of a home area for older children who often need the security of a setting in which they are free to play out their feelings and emotions. During an expressive arts session in the first week of a PGCE primary course we saw how all children need opportunities to play out their experiences.

We had invited children from a range of schools to take part in workshops in art, drama, music, story and technology. One of the most revealing moments came after lunch when children were playing in both outside and indoor spaces. A Year 3 group had their lunch in an early years base and spied the home area. They quickly took over and used tables, chairs and cooking facilities as they became small children, parents, relatives and visiting trades-men. Their involvement in this play was of a quality far beyond anything they had shown in their workshops and made us realise the power and value of imaginative role play at all ages.

That is not to say that every junior classroom needs a home area, but some opportunities for role play outside the more struc-tured activities of the classroom would be of value, as we shall see in future examples.

Home area materials

Cooking and eating equipment
Child-sized sink, stove, refrigerator
Adult-sized forks, spoons, knives, chop-
    sticks
Cooking containers – pots, pans, wok, rice
    cooker
Cooking tools –
    barbeque cooking utensils
    slotted spoons, spatulas, ladles
    eggbeater, whisk, food mill, mortar and
        pestle
    sandtimer, bell timer
    teapot, coffeepot
    colander, sieves
    ice-cube trays
    cookie press and cutters
    hamburger press, tortilla press
    can opener
Baking equipment –
    cake pans, muffin pans, loaf pans
    mixing bowls and lids
    measuring cups and spoons
    rolling pin
    sifter
    canister set
Dishes – plates, bowls, cups, saucers
Sponges, dishcloths, towels, potholders
Tablecloths, placemats, napkins
Things to cook and serve – seeds, seed
    pods, beans, shells, stones, pine
    cones, chestnuts, acorns, macaroni,
    noodles, buttons, bottle caps, poker
    chips, Styrofoam packing pieces, fabric
    squares for wrapping
Empty food containers – boxes, cans, car-
    tons, jars, and bags, with original lables
    in English, Japanese, Arabic, Spanish,
    and so forth to reflect children's home
    languages

Pretending and role-play materials
Dolls – female and male, commercial and
    home-made, to reflect the skin colors,
    hair styles, facial features and special
    needs of children in the program
Stuffed animals
Doll beds, blankets, stroller, front/back
    pack
Baby rattles, bibs, bottles, diapers, clothes
    (pants and dresses)
Broom, dustpan
Toaster (wooden or de-electrified), clocks
    (wind-up or de-electrified)

Mirror
Two telephones
Small stepladder
Dress-up clothes and accessories – hats,
    shoes, purses, wallets, briefcases,
    scarves, head wraps, jewelry, masks,
    neckties, belts, suspenders
Lunch boxes, picnic basket, laundry bas-
    ket
Toolbox and tools
Envelopes, canceled stamps, seals, stick-
    ers, junk mail
Typewriter, keyboard
Sturdy cardboard boxes
Low, moveable partitions
Props –
    home-builders' props: toolbox, tools,
        empty paint cans, brushes, pipe fit-
        tings
    doctors' props: lab coats, Band-Aids,
        gauze, stethoscope, cloth bandages
    farm props: overalls, pail, straw, animal
        brush, empty feed bag
    gas-station props: empty oil can, hose,
        rags, empty past-wax can, jack, lug
        wrench, steering wheel, hubcaps
    fire-station props: hats, raincoats,
        boots, hoses
    restaurant props: hats, aprons, cups,
        straws, napkins, menus, order pads
        and pencils
    fishing props: fishing poles, nets, heavy
        boots, sou'westers, buckets, oars,
        gas can, buoys

Homelike materials
Rocking chair or easy chair
Blankets, sheets, quilts, pillows, beach
    towels, sleeping bags
Photos of program's children and their
    families
Wall hangings reflecting local community
Real plants, watering can

*Real cooking equipment (stored out of chil-
dren's reach and used only with an adult
present)*
Hotplate, toaster oven
Electric frying pan
Popcorn popper with clear lid

Reference photos and recipes
Cookbooks, picture recipes
Field-trip photos (for role-play ideas)

Figure 2.1 Home area materials (Hohmann and Weikhart 1995, p. 131)

Several writers have suggested settings for play based on different themes or topics, for example Hall and Abbott (1991) and Hall and Robinson (1995). The term 'role-play areas' is also used by Hendy (1994) to describe setting up thematic play for children to explore in different ways. There are many possible play areas which can be developed arising from topics used to develop the curriculum. The following list is by no means exhaustive, but suggests possible themes:

- post office;
- doctor's surgery or hospital;
- fire station;
- police station;
- lifeboat;
- space rocket;
- aeroplane;
- clothes or shoe shop;
- greengrocers;
- garden centre;
- garage;
- pirate ship;
- ocean liner;
- hairdressers;
- fitness studio;
- photographic/film/ recording studio;
- office;
- bank;
- Victorian kitchen;
- jungle/rainforest;
- information centre/ travel agent;
- castle;
- cave;
- cafe/restaurant.

CASE STUDIES

The spaceship (I): Reception/Year 1

A topic on Space is often very popular with this age group and provides many opportunities for learning. Providing a role-play area 'inside a spaceship' gives children the chance to demonstrate freely what they might have understood from all their studies. In this example, the theme of space had been part of the work of the class for about three weeks. Children had created a moonscape, a planet frieze, 3-D rockets, a countdown and a large collage of an alien, and had carried out many kinds of writing. Inside the rocket, silver foil had been used to line the inner walls, and there was a control panel and a planning backboard. The children could wear space suits, helmets and cylinders for oxygen, the props suggesting the kind of play that might occur. There was also a log book for children to fill in as they wished.

Resources

The materials were all provided by the teachers and they had set up the role-play area for the children to come into as a surprise. The children were used to having a role-play area and knew they would all have opportunities to play in it in small groups. Additional objects were added arising from discussions with the children, such as large jars with different kinds of food measured on the jar for each day.

Research

There were many books around relating to space, both fact and fiction. There were also newspaper and magazine cuttings, children's own books of information and a computer program of a space story.

Children's contributions

Parents knew about the topic and encouraged children's interest in news reports. There was always something from the children during their news or review time which added information for the whole class.

Assessing value

Photographs of some of the play episodes were discussed with the children. They often reported back on their play episodes or looked at their own books or the log book which was kept in the rocket. Further examples of how the activities were evaluated by the teachers are considered in the next chapter.

The tourist information centre: a whole-school project

This arose from a topic on the local environment. It was a whole-school topic and the role-play area was used by children aged from four through to eleven in a village school of 120 pupils. The area was set up in a small resources room which was reorganised to provide one table, chairs, shelves, a notice board, a computer and printer, a concept keyboard and overlays, a cashdesk and a telephone. A parent loaned an old fax and answer machine for the duration of the topic.

Resources

Most of these were collected and made by the children. They included maps of parts of the local area, published maps, leaflets, postcards, large posters of popular places and advertisements. All classes did their own versions of postcards, maps, leaflets and membership cards. Booking forms were designed and produced on the computer.

Research

Each class made a visit to a local information centre and collected and discussed maps, leaflets and guidebooks.

Teacher input

Teachers occasionally observed children in the centre but usually a non-teaching assistant was in the area and was alert to any issues which arose. Teachers added materials or encouraged children to do so when ideas came from the children or as part of whole-school planning, for example including information needed for characters from children's literature.

Assessing value

All classes had opportunities to play in the centre and to take on roles such as visitors, children, parents, information officers and creatures from another planet. On some occasions the activities were left to the children and they used the area as they wished. At other times children worked out questions for the information they required. They also used characters from books so that on some days all their play centred on what certain characters might wish to know, for example what information might Toad, Ratty and Mole from *The Wind in the Willows* require for their travels? Teachers were able to assess speaking and listening and written responses and sometimes discuss children's activities as part of their review times.

The ocean liner: Year 4

Resources
Children were involved in setting up this area by painting portholes and making the ship's wheel and navigation instruments. They produced a guide to the ship, tourist maps and guides of different journeys, a ship's menu and a list of activities and entertainment for each day. There were dressing-up clothes available, including uniforms and clothes for different activities.

Research
The children researched places to stop, climatic conditions, navigation, shipping forecasts, how ships work and how to plan time distances.

Children's contributions
In addition to the resources listed above, the children made brochures and postcards. They compiled lists of items they would take with them for different journeys, and made passports. They also made sunglasses, binoculars and hats and drew and collected photographs of one another on holiday.

Teacher input
The teacher encouraged the collection and making of resources, and added additional materials as and when required.

Assessing value
Each group of five or six children planned their journeys to cover one or two weeks. These were discussed in review time. Children also reported back on weather, incidents and things they enjoyed most. The teacher observed the play in the play area, recording as necessary.

The recording studio: Year 5

My name is George Spikes. I am going to tell you a joke. What has six legs, two eyes, three ears and no feet?

Give up?

I don't know, but it's crawling up your leg.

The fun of telling jokes and rhymes and hearing them recorded was one of the incidental activities of the role-play area developed as a recording studio. A class of nine-year-olds were engaged in a topic on sound. It had been decided to create a recording studio in a bay outside the classroom so that two classes could make use of it. An assortment of tape recorders, microphones headphones, a working telephone and an old record player had been assembled, as well as a computer with CD-ROM and printer, notepads and pens.

As part of the overall curriculum planning, children from each class worked in small groups to produce musical sequences using instruments kept in another musical area. They also took on roles for interviewing, writing plans for programmes and deciding the timing of various recordings.

When individual groups came to the bay they had usually made a plan for what they would do and how they would use the equipment. One group of six children decided to concentrate on publicity and made posters of what the studio could offer. Another group prepared a series of interviews of favourite singers or writers. Others prepared individual talks or conversations based on interests and hobbies. Gradually, as the topic developed, the activities became more focused as children went to the play area with very clear ideas about what they would do and achieve.

Throughout the topic children were working on different aspects of sound. They were learning about the physical processes of vibration and sound, which included experimenting with pitch and loudness, and they were putting these ideas into practice in their use of musical instruments for composing and also in their use of sounds to set a character or mood. The children had also had opportunities to share their skills in using talk for a variety of purposes such as descriptions, reporting events, conversations, arguments and interviews.

All of these activities will be familiar to many teachers who have developed topics which have drawn upon the key skills in different curriculum areas. What may not be quite so familiar is the play dimension which enabled children to use their skills in their own chosen ways. Although the outcomes were presented to the rest of the class, the interactions between children as they developed their sequences gave them opportunities to explore, select and reject their own versions of what was recorded. One group chose to present interviews:

John:	Good morning, good morning and what do we have today?
Jane:	Is that what you are going to put on? It's not in the plan.
John:	No, but it sounds like the radio in the morning.
Jane:	Sarah, you have got the plan. What does it say?
Sarah:	Music – slow from tape for the ship sinking and people feeling sad. Andrew interview ship's captain – two minutes.
	Music, it doesn't say what. Jokes John.
John:	You see I can make it funny if I want to.
Sarah:	Then it's me, Jane and then you.
Jane:	I think we should try the music and then go through each one.
John:	And I can be the introducer.
Andrew:	Yes, but you have to stay within the timing. Let's run through our bits first.
Sarah:	Yes, then we can fit in the music and John if there is time.
John:	Oh no, OK.

There were a number of important experiences emerging through this group's interactions. They were very aware of the timing required to put all the different aspects together. They were able to argue, cooperate, use technical vocabulary, share ideas, imagine feelings, and use equipment in a competent way, taking on board what they had seen and heard of the characteristics of recording and their knowledge of sound and communication. They became much more confident in putting their ideas across and in using what they knew. Here was an episode of play where the setting and materials were structured, yet children made it their own, developed their own scenarios and were able to use more of their knowledge than might have been possible within the classroom setting.

Starting any of these topics takes planning and preparation, but once under way they can provide many opportunities for children to try out and experiment with their knowledge. It would be unrealistic to suggest that every play episode in these examples was purposeful or enabled children to extend their learning, but what they did provide was freedom for children to interpret these themes in their own way and relate them to what they already knew. Again, children were in control but there were opportunities for them to be challenged by the theme. Thematic play areas are another way of enabling children to reflect their knowledge and show how they were making sense of it in a setting which was focused yet free. How we as teachers interpret children's play episodes will be considered in the next chapter.

Summary

We have argued that play has a long tradition as part of the primary school curriculum and has been seen as a valuable vehicle for active learning and as a means of enabling children to go beyond their concrete learning into more imaginative realms. We have considered what is meant by structure in the play which occurs in classrooms and the advantages of loose structure in providing children with opportunities to clarify their understandings. The final examples show how play can provide additional support for the themes and topics of classroom learning and be part of the planning of the overall curriculum. Future chapters discuss how these opportunities may provide children with the contexts in which they can come to terms with the cognitive challenges which arise through their classroom learning and ways in which teachers can observe and evaluate what is taking place.

CHAPTER 3

How do we Find Out What Children Learn Through Play?

Holly Griffin has argued that in play: 'If the activity of children is viewed as an aspect of distinct child culture rather than as a precursor of adult abilities, questions can focus on describing the activity from the point of view of the actors' (1984, p. 75).

This chapter poses the question of how we find out what children think about their play and how teachers might assess and understand children's responses. It is divided into three parts:

- research which has been carried out on children's own observations of their play;
- some strategies for classroom observations which enable teachers to observe what children think they are doing when they play;
- implications of these observations for children's learning and teachers' planning.

We begin by looking at what we know about children's perceptions of their play and what they think they are doing when they are presented with opportunities to play in classroom settings. This may not be quite as adults imagine when they turn to it from the perspectives of the children.

In a study of three infant classrooms in 1978, the sociologist Ronald King found that children's perceptions of play were not the same as those of their teachers. For example, playing in the sand was seen by children as 'playing at sandcastles', while teachers saw it as building up concepts as a preparation for doing mathematics. Teachers viewed play as a natural activity for young children but they also defined the play activities for them. King (1978, p. 21) made the point that the kind of play being defined arose from the way teachers presented the different resources available in the classroom and their intentions for children's learning.

A very revealing discussion of how children view their play arose in a study of 15 five- and six-year-old Swedish children. Karrby (1989) was particularly interested in children talking about what they were doing rather than she as the researcher making observations of their activities. The children were asked to talk about what they had been doing, about their intentions, what they had learned and if their play was connected to learning. Karrby compared children's descriptions of their pretend play with discussions of more structured learning experiences. When the children talked about what it meant to play and what it meant to learn, they associated play with activities involving pretend and fantasy and gave much richer descriptions of these activities. This type of play accounted for 10 per cent of the activities in the Swedish pre-school and was closely related to dialogue conversation and small-group organisation.

In Karrby's study children saw play as a whole event often based on a theme such as a robbery or a party. They only used the term 'play' to refer to pretend or dramatic play which had been agreed by themselves. They gave detailed accounts of how the play emerged, who played what role, the rules and what was allowed or not allowed, so that the play was seen as a whole sequence. As one child commented, 'in my fantasy activity, you have to think for yourself'. When they talked about their activities it became clear that for these children construction play or the mastery of physical skills were not really playing. They defined these activities as 'doing things such as building something or practising something to be good at it'. Karrby concludes that: 'A better understanding of what affective forces and strategies are revealed in play may give us a clearer picture of the development of cognitive processes. A valuable tool in this respect is interviewing children.' (1989, p. 54)

The symbolic or make-believe aspects of play are particularly important for children in the behaviours they think of as play.

Pellegrini and Galda (1993) reviewed a range of studies about play and concluded that being able to choose an activity might not mean it is perceived as play unless it can be developed as children wish. When we examine how older children describe their play, the imaginative/fantasy aspect is again mentioned by them but interpreted in different ways. A group of nine- to eleven-year-olds explained that 'play is what the young ones do when they are Thunderbirds'.

They viewed their own play as a much more sophisticated form of activity, such as copying adverts and interviewing one another as if on TV, including making jokes and mimicking popular personalities. They remembered adverts and were able to use different voices to get their meaning across. A theme with a structure and rules was considered to be an important component of the play. Indeed they spent much of their time planning their play and how it would develop before it actually got underway: 'We always talk about what we will do first.'

Evaluating play activities

If we are to take play seriously as part of the learning which takes place in classrooms, we need to make sure that it is included in the overall planning and that time is spent in observing the insights it may reveal. Figure 3.1 shows the planning and assessment cycle in which play can be a part.

Observing children when they play is a valuable part of recording their progress and gaining insights into their understandings. This cannot always happen when children are actually engaged in their play, so we need to draw on strategies which enable teachers to think about the information they collect at a later time. The following approaches have been found to be productive for collecting information and evaluating children's learning:
- dramatic representations;
- recall or review;
- photographs which may later be discussed by the children;
- video and audio recording while children are engaged in play;
- written accounts or drawings of the play;
- mapping the pattern or sequence of what took place;
- diaries of the way play developed.

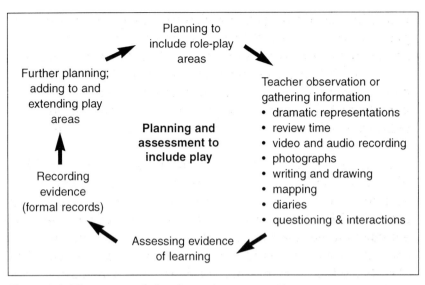

Figure 3.1 Play as part of planning and assessment

These ideas for finding out how children are interpreting their activities are not new. The following examples show how such strategies have been developed in the classroom to give insights on how children are making sense of their play activities.

Observations of dramatic representations in play episodes

The dramatic representation or acting out of particular themes and roles is seen as play by children of all ages. In her insightful book *Wally's Stories,* Gussin Paley (1981) described children 'acting out' their dictated stories and the motivation this gave them for inventing and having their stories written down. She encouraged her kindergarten children to use their pictures to dramatise the stories they dictated to their teacher. Wally dictated: 'The dinosaur smashed down the city and the people got mad and put him in jail. He promised he would be good so they let him go home and his mother was waiting' (1981, p. 12); Paley observed that writing the words down for the children was not enough: 'the words did not sufficiently represent the action which needed to be shared. For this *dramatic representation* alone, the children would give up play time, as it was a true extension of play' (1981, p. 12).

This 'acting out' of a story can be a stimulating part of review times when children might wish to dramatise an episode they have written about or played or an aspect of a story they have enjoyed.

CASE STUDIES

Macbeth

For older children the process of dramatising a story or event is worthwhile as it gives them a chance to get into the role of another person and have some empathy with the character and events being depicted. A group of nine- and ten-year-olds were involved in acting out their own version of *Macbeth* as part of a historical project on the Tudors. They worked with a drama teacher who presented them with the story, gave out parts and encouraged them to use their own words as well as the Shakespearean text in order to put across the meaning. The children put on the play in a local Tudor mansion. During the performance they moved between four rooms, including one with a gallery. The audience moved around with the actors to follow the story. This all involved a high level of organisation for the children in developing their roles in an authentic setting.

In discussing the value of this experience they were all very positive about it and adamant that this involved much work and could not be seen as just playing. They pointed out that they had to do a lot of research on the costumes for the play, the food for the Elizabethan banquet and other props. They had to get the feel of the play itself – the theme and plot. They had to learn the words and their positioning on the set and were engaged in acting out their roles in imaginative ways. They saw this as drama which was quite distinct from what they thought of as 'play', although they did acknowledge their enjoyment in playing out individual roles and building up to the final performance. Many of the group agreed that the experience was both 'work' and 'fun':

> Why I thought it was work was because I was learning about Macbeth. What happened in the play was that Macbeth would have been King after Macduff died. He was so impatient that he killed the King.

> It was fun acting out the play. I felt quite proud of myself.

John Cabot (I)

In another school, ten- and eleven-year-olds who were putting on a play about John Cabot were very clear that for them this was play, because of their own involvement and control of the dramatisation. They had discussed and chosen characters and had written the play, including their own jokes from popular culture. This had then been put together by their teachers and they were now interpreting the script. Developing the actions and finding suitable costumes were all done by them with a little advice from their teachers. They felt so much in control they were adamant that this was play because they were so much a part of the way it was all evolving. They did acknowledge that there were work elements in a project they were doing on Bristol which gave them the background for the play:

'I have learnt a lot more about Bristol and the life of the sailors in those times.'

The children felt that although they knew themselves very well they had gained much more experience of working together as a team. This arose in their singing and in the actions which formed part of the play (Figure 3.2).

Figure 3.2 Preparing to sail

Overall this drama experience involved:
- researching information on the historical background of John Cabot and his voyage;
- researching costumes and customs of the time;
- finding out about life on the Matthew;
- visiting a replica of the ship when it was in the harbour;
- writing their parts;
- learning and improvising the script;
- improvising movements;
- learning sea shanties and dances such as the hornpipe;
- cooperating with one another in the scenes, songs and dances;
- appreciating one anothers' special skills.

There was much cooperation and empathy which went way beyond the National Curriculum and yet would fulfil many of the requirements for English, History, Geography, Music and PE.

In both examples these junior-aged children had made the transition from sociodramatic play through to drama as a result of their involvement and shaping of the topics and stories they were acting out.

Teachers were able to make assessments of the dramatic representations of these older children through looking at the ideas and language used in their written script. The children were quite happy for their teachers to produce the overall script from all their ideas, which they then discussed and made further amendments to. The discussion was recorded by the teachers and used to observe how children cooperated with one another and demonstrated their understandings of some of the ideas in the play.

Myra: Do you think they would ask the Captain if they could have some more food?

Sara: No, I do not think so, they would be too scared.

Joanna: Yes, and they were very poor so they would just be glad to be on the ship.

Dan: But if you were hungry and you had hungry children you might and you would not mind the weevils.

Sara: Hmm, maybe. Shall we put it in anyway?

This kind of exchange helps teachers to know what children have understood from their research and their awareness of the dilemmas which occurred in such situations. Preparing for the drama also helped teachers to decide if the process was useful and how they might improve on it on another occasion.

Review or recall

In order to know how children are responding to opportunities for play and learning, we need to observe their actions and interactions with one another as they play. One way in which teachers are able to confirm their own observations and gain insights into what play has meant to children is the review time which many organise at the end of sessions.

Review or recall time originated in the High/Scope Curriculum Model which includes the organisational strategies of 'plan, do, review'. When children first start in nursery schools or classes or in reception classes they often engage in activities such as drawing, painting, construction or role play. They are encouraged to recall what they have been doing during a session and talk about their experiences clearly to the rest of their group. For example: 'I played with Tinkertoys and made some of those lifter things.'

In High/Scope terms: 'Recalling involves social interaction on a very personal level – reflecting on experiences and finding the words, actions and gestures to convey clear meanings to others' (Hohmann and Weikart 1995, p. 227).

Review, in the High/Scope sense, really begins when children begin to reflect on how effective their plans and activities have been: 'I got a long Tinkertoy for the lifter and then put the round wheel things on for the weights.' During review time teachers can intervene to clarify children's understandings and help them to articulate their ideas: 'Where did you stand to lift the things?'

The following example took place in a nursery school where children 'planned' what they wished to do and this was followed by 'work' time when they carried out their plan in different areas of the room. This enabled their teacher, Sue, to spend some time in observing one child so that she could provide support during review time and remind the child of what she may have made or been doing during her 'work' time. The opportunity for children to review what they had done enabled Sue then to be further aware of individual levels of understanding and to record any significant achievement.

CASE STUDY

The ballet

Ann and Sarah, aged four, are reviewing their plan for the morning with the aid of Sue. Sue has made observations of Ann during 'work' time and she concentrates on extending her language. The day before they all made a visit to the ballet. Ann and Sarah had planned to do some dancing like the ballet they had seen.

Sue:	Can you remember your plan, Ann?
Ann:	Yes, I did the ballet with Sarah but we didn't really have time as me and Sarah was getting ready and I was sitting and Sarah said I couldn't have a dress but I just stopped wearing it.
Sue:	Did you go to the resources area with Ann to do your dancing?
Sarah:	No, I danced with Tom.
Sue:	Sarah danced with Tom – what about you Ann, did you do some dancing when you got there?
Ann:	I didn't but I listened to some nice music in the resources area. I don't know what the music was called though.
Sue:	I don't suppose I do. Do you know what it was like? What sort of music was it that you were listening to?
Ann:	I didn't really. I didn't really want it on so loud but I put it on so loud I couldn't really hear it.

Sue: You did put it on very loud.

Ann: Yes, but I put it on so loud that I didn't even believe how loud the music was. I thought it was even too louder.

Sue: Were you listening to it with the headset or were you listening to it just with the tape recorder?

Ann: Just with the tape recorder but I really wanted the headphones and I didn't get them at all.

Sue: Did you know there is a button on the tape recorder that you can turn to make the sound quieter?

Ann: Yes. I put them both on but they were very loud.

Sue: Can you tell us, was the music fast or slow?

Ann: I think it was slow.

Sarah: Was it my music?

Ann: There wasn't any fast ballet and there wasn't any time to do ballet was there Sarah?

Sue: What sort of dancing did you do?

Sarah: We did twirls like this. Went right up on my toes. I didn't have enough time and flicked my skirt like this.

Sue: Could you show us a twirl? And another one ... and another one. A twirl in ballet is a pirouette. Did you go all the way round when you did your twirl?

Experiencing the ballet has given the girls a chance to imagine themselves in the role of ballet dancers and to notice speed and pace in music. Their opportunities to use language varies, but being encouraged to describe their activities at length enables them to show what they have remembered and helps Sue to extend their thinking. Spending time talking about the tape recorder with Ann ensures some understanding for both Ann and other children in the group who were listening if not participating. Sue's question, 'Can you tell us, was the music fast or slow?', really makes Ann think. She not only understands soft and loud but is able to make a further judgement, 'I think it was slow', and when Sarah says 'Was it my music?' Ann responds and confirms the speed: 'There wasn't any fast ballet and there wasn't any time to do ballet was there Sarah?'

In spite of the concentration on Ann to ensure her development of meanings, there are also opportunities for Sarah to be part of the conversation. Although she does not say much at the beginning, Sarah is mentioned by Ann and included by Sue when she asks, 'Did you go to the resources area with Ann to do your dancing?' Sarah replies, 'No I danced with Tom'. This short exchange means that Sarah continues to feel involved in the whole conversation, so much so that towards the end of the episode she is able to interject as we saw above: 'Was it my music?'

The turn taking and conversational devices used by the two girls are at quite a sophisticated level. Their use of language is also encouraged by Sue, who supports Ann in developing meaning through her talk and in extending her reasoning skills. Ann is able to use causation very well in several of her responses, again encouraged by Sue's subtly focused and enabling questioning:

Teacher: Were you listening to it with the headset or were you listening to it just with the tape recorder?

Ann: Just with the tape recorder but I really wanted the headphones and I didn't get them at all.

There is a conversation going on here which encourages the children to think about their activities and reflect on what has taken place. Sue also ensures that the children's vocabulary is extended when she encourages Sarah to demonstrate her dancing:

Sue: Could you show us a twirl? And another one ... and another one. A twirl in ballet is a pirouette. Did you go all the way round when you did your twirl?

Here new vocabulary is introduced, reminding the children again of their experiences of seeing the dancing the previous day and relating it to their own attempts at what they describe as 'twirls'.

Commenting on this review time Sue shows that much more was gained from the session than she had first anticipated:

Initially I had two main aims for the session. I intended to develop the children's personal and social skills, their ability to enable one child to take her turn and to share her experiences and so of course to develop listening skills. The other aim was to focus on Ann and to extend her language skills – her ability to listen and to report, reason, predict and use vocabulary. However, I felt much more was gained from the session in other ways. I learned about Ann's ability to talk about music and dance, about the tape recorder and about how she spent her time. This was particularly valuable as in previous review sessions she has tended to focus on the concrete items she has made, revealing quite different skills and knowledge.

This one taped review session also provided the teacher with evidence of Ann's ability to achieve the Desirable Outcomes. In Language and Literacy she was able to: 'listen attentively; talk about her experiences, express thoughts and explore meanings using an increasing vocabulary'; in her 'Knowledge and Understanding of the World' she was able to 'question why things happen and how things work, look closely at similarities and differences and talk about her observations' (SCAA 1996, pp. 3–4), to name but a few!

Young children often need support in forming sentences and language and organising their ideas. As a result of their work with the reception teachers, Bennett *et al.* suggest that the success of review times 'depends on children learning a repertoire of social and cognitive skills to engage in metacognitive reflection' (1997, p. 126).

Providing a structure for review times is a means of encouraging children to be more consciously aware of what they have been learning and achieving in their play. The following are some ideas which have been effective in promoting successful recall:

- looking at photographs of different activity areas so that the children can pick out the order of their activities;
- reminding them of interactions – 'Where did you play?', 'Who was playing with you?';
- making a chart of the areas and asking them to draw a picture of themselves in whichever area they were in; this can be made more sophisticated with diagrams of the areas which children fill in showing their progress to different activities during the session;
- asking them to act out their play in a particular area;
- asking them to bring an item they have drawn or made to show other children and about which the other children can ask questions;
- inviting them to ask questions of one another – 'Would anyone like to ask Ann another question about her dancing?';
- framing responses – 'Think about how you will start to tell us what you did in the science area'.

Enabling children to review their activities or the themes of their play can be a useful way of encouraging and extending their language skills. A teacher working with a Year 1 class found children needed strategies to help them recall what had taken place. She encouraged the children to talk in pairs about one play activity they had engaged in or one thing they had made during the session. As with some of the ideas above this took a while to establish, but it did mean that children were more focused when they reviewed their activities with the whole group.

Reviewing *Macbeth*

The range of National Curriculum requirements for Speaking and Listening in English at Key Stage 2 states:

> Pupils should be given opportunities to talk for a range of purposes, including:
> - exploring, developing and explaining ideas;
> - planning, predicting and investigating;
> - sharing ideas, insights and opinions;
> - reading aloud, telling and enacting stories and poems;

- reporting and describing events and observations;
- presenting to audiences, live and on tape.

Pupils should be given opportunities to communicate to different audiences and to reflect on how speakers adapt their vocabulary, tone, pace and style.

Pupils should be given opportunities to listen and respond to a range of people. They should be taught to identify and comment on key features of what they see and hear in a variety of media.

Pupils should be given opportunities to participate in a wide range of drama activities, including improvisation, role play and the writing and performance of scripted drama. In responding to drama, they should be encouraged to evaluate their own and others' contributions. (DfE 1995, p. 11)

The children who had taken part in *Macbeth* had a more sophisticated use of language than the younger children when reviewing their activities and covered many aspects of the requirements. In thinking about their experiences they listened to others and were able to make relevant contributions to the discussions. They were able to reflect on what they had learnt and articulate their feelings using appropriate discourse:

I really liked my part because the costume made everything more realistic as well as the setting.

I remembered all my words and found it very easy on the night but I felt very scared on stage and when I spoke I felt like that person but it was very lifelike.

The only thing I didn't like about it was that I didn't get to say all my words because someone came on when I was meant to.

They remembered learning their lines and being able to improvise the Shakespearean language:

Most of the time we used modern-day words and put them into a form that we could understand.

Simon observed:

There were some parts I got stuck on like 'despair thy charm, and know Macduff was from his mother's womb untimely ripp'd' which was where I got 'untimely' and 'ripp'd' confused.

Robert declared:

> Macbeth was one of the greatest things I have ever done. I had to
> practise night and day to get it spot on.

A little dramatic, but nevertheless showing the effort he felt he
had put into the experience. Several of the children reflected their
feelings about the parts they had been given. Janet, who played
Lady Macbeth, gave a very honest appraisal:

> I do fit Lady Macbeth's part – bossy, impatient, overpowering.
> When I got the part I was absolutely delighted.'

David also showed he had thought a lot about his character and
the way he behaved in the play:

> I was Banquo and I felt that the play was a little weird because one
> minute I'm Macbeth's friend and the next minute he kills me. I
> liked my part though because it was gruesome. It was gruesome
> because I had so much stage blood.

Others commented about playing a role in a play in the authentic
Tudor setting and showed just how much this authenticity meant
in enabling them to feel they were engaging in something worthwhile:

> I felt as if I was a proper person in it.
> It felt like I was really part of it and it was a really good feeling.

All of these children were reflecting their understandings of
working together as part of a dramatic production. The play element for them was the fun they had in doing *Macbeth* for their
parents and friends and being given the opportunity to perform
in a real Tudor setting. Their reflection on their performances
showed the cognitive, affective and social dimensions of their
learning as they came to more of an awareness of 'Life in Tudor
Times', one of the study units for Key Stage 2 history. The drama
of the role play enabled them to have greater empathy with the
characters and more realistic experiences of the language, costumes, food and customs of the time.

Photographs as prompts

While we can appreciate that not all episodes of play may always
seem purposeful in adult terms, it is worth looking at play which
occurs over time.

CASE STUDY

The spaceship (II)

The reception class who were involved in the project on space had a role-play area – inside a spaceship. Initially the play was exploratory, as children began to appreciate the possibilities in the area. It was suggested to them that they might wish to plan a journey to one of the planets and this idea quickly caught on. Over a period of three weeks the play varied depending on the combinations of children and their particular interests.

The teachers hoped that the play would allow children to consolidate many of the ideas and information about space that they had talked about and looked at in books. They also hoped that children would collaborate with one another, use technical language and experiment with their own ideas about space as they understood it. Although the teachers did not directly observe what was taking place, they were able to pick up much that was happening by working close by with other children, through the children's comments in review time, and through the use of drawings and photographs, which enabled them to talk with the children about their play even though they had not seen it. One group, looking at the pictures, had already identified that the room they were in was for group work or for play and were able to make some distinctions between work and play activities:

Teacher: So everything in the spaceship was playing?

Sammy: No, look up there, the planets, we talked about them and put the names on with our teacher.

Sammy had noticed the frieze of planets and was able to identify it as an activity set up for making and naming planets, which was different to the play he experienced inside the spaceship (Figure 3.3).

The teachers' purposes emerged in the way the children planned for their play. One group began by cleaning the board followed by one child doing a countdown. All began drawing planets on the board (Figure 3.4).

G: Which planet are we going to?

B: We can't go to a hot place?

S: Let's go to Jupiter.

G: Yes.

B: No, that is the hottest planet, that one further away.

S: Uranus, that's not too near the Sun.

In using the names of planets, some of their knowledge was being reiterated. They were also discussing and giving logical reasons for their decisions. On a later occasion the same group of children built on their previous play episode (Figure 3.5):

Figure 3.3 The frieze of planets above the spaceship

Figure 3.4
Preparing for 'lift-off'

Figure 3.5 Walking the dog on the moon

Figure 3.6 In the shower

B:	7.6.5.4.3.2.1. Lift off.
S:	We are not ready yet, we don't know where we are going.
B:	Yes we do – Saturn – it's pink and yellow.
E:	I'm going to have a walk on the moon. I'll take the dog.
B:	Alright.

What was interesting about the play of many of the group was that they linked it up with what the spaceship had been previously:

E: First it was just an ordinary house and then a vet and now a spaceship.

John and Elizabeth had enjoyed dressing up as space people and getting into a small cupboard (Figure 3.6). In looking at the photographs, they had their different interpretations:

John: Just at the bottom of Saturn there is a shower would be coming down and I was looking at the water.
Elizabeth: Yes, it was to get mud off when walking on the moon.

Elizabeth also referred back to the shower:

Elizabeth: I thought of the dog shower. I just decided to be a dog.

Elements of the present and previous themes were evident in the play of all the groups. They made drinks and washed things in a washing machine as well as acting as astronauts. Several of the groups had a space dog which was taken for walks on the moon.

It was G's birthday, and a party was held in the spaceship and elements of home play were again drawn on, emphasising observations that home play is one of the most common kinds of pretend play children engaged in (Pellegrini 1984). This also showed how much the play is under the children's own control and how they can experiment with the themes as they wish, so making the play particular to them. These children were using their imaginative play to show what they knew about planets, to collaborate with one another, and to control their activities; they were also bringing to it classroom knowledge and outside knowledge. Even though the context had been set they did not always stay with the play theme suggested but used it as a framework for the kinds of activities they wished to engage in.

Videoing play

In another case, teachers had videoed six-year-old children who were reflecting their experiences in the dialogues taking place between them.

CASE STUDY

The Sunshine City church

Inside the area set up as a church in Sunshine City, a boy and a girl approach the table. Another child takes on the role of vicar.

Vicar:	Do you take her to be your lawful wedded wife?
Justin:	No. No.
Vicar:	You have got to say it – yes.
Justin:	No.
Vicar:	Right. Get out.
	(*The children leave and return with two other children, one dressed as a policewoman.*)
Girl:	Justin, I can't get bridesmaids.
Vicar:	Now you have got to marry her. Justin do you take her to be your lawful wedded wife?
Justin:	No.
Girl:	You have to say it with Naomi.
Vicar:	Naomi, do you take her to be your lawful wedded wife?
Naomi:	Yes.
Vicar:	(*shouts*) Great. I have got someone to be the lawful wedded wife.

In spite of some confusion these children are playing out their experiences of weddings. The props, language and behaviour are all used to provide a framework in which they are able to vary the content according to their wishes. The episode also shows the multiple levels of meaning which can occur as children interact with one another and bring their individual experiences and interpretations to their play, for example, 'You have to say it with Naomi', a memory of some of the structure of the marriage ceremony.

1. Turn taking
   - who speaks first?
   - whose utterances are longer or shorter?
   - who controls the conversation?

2. Relationships between speakers
   - how do speakers address each other?

3. Vocabulary and grammatical choices
   - is there any technical or topic vocabulary or terminology used?
   - what kinds of utterances are used? Question, answer, statement?

4. Paralinguistic features
   - actions, pace, tone, tempo;
   - repeats, pauses, intonation patterns.

Figure 3.7 A framework for analysis (Language in the National Curriculum, 1993, p. 226)

The teachers involved used the episode to look at the speaking and listening skills of the children, and were interested in the 'turn taking' which occurred. Figure 3.7 shows aspects which are worth considering when analysing the conversations in play episodes.

The children speak with confidence and choose appropriate vocabulary with precision, as in 'lawful wedded wife'. The children's use of intonation and apparent understanding of an aspect of their culture – a wedding – emerges through their language and the actions taking place. The boy playing the vicar knows what is expected and the important line which constitutes his role. It is only when the second girl arrives and is able to find a substitute for Justin that the ceremony can continue. In this episode the turn taking is encouraged by the boy playing the vicar, who not only asks appropriate questions but prompts others through his statements: 'You have got to say it – yes.' The pace, tempo and intonation patterns are all appropriate and maintained between speakers.

Written accounts or drawings of the play

This is a common strategy for assessing children's experiences and is helpful in showing any significant understandings of what has occurred. The children playing in the spaceship did a number of unsolicited drawings and books of their play. At a very simple level, just three pictures gave an indication of what the play had meant to Jane (Figure 3.8), while Sammy's wish on a star, 'I wish for my mam and dad to have a rasig cr' (Figure 3.9), was carefully considered and he was keen to talk about it when playing in the spaceship.

Figure 3.8 Space pictures

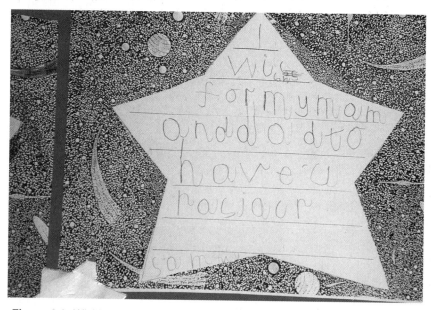

Figure 3.9 Wishing on a star

The children working on *Macbeth* wrote about their experiences
with enthusiasm and were also keen to draw their interpretations

of parts of the experiences. The use of language had made a strong impression on some of them who were able to record their parts within the whole activity (Figure 3.10).

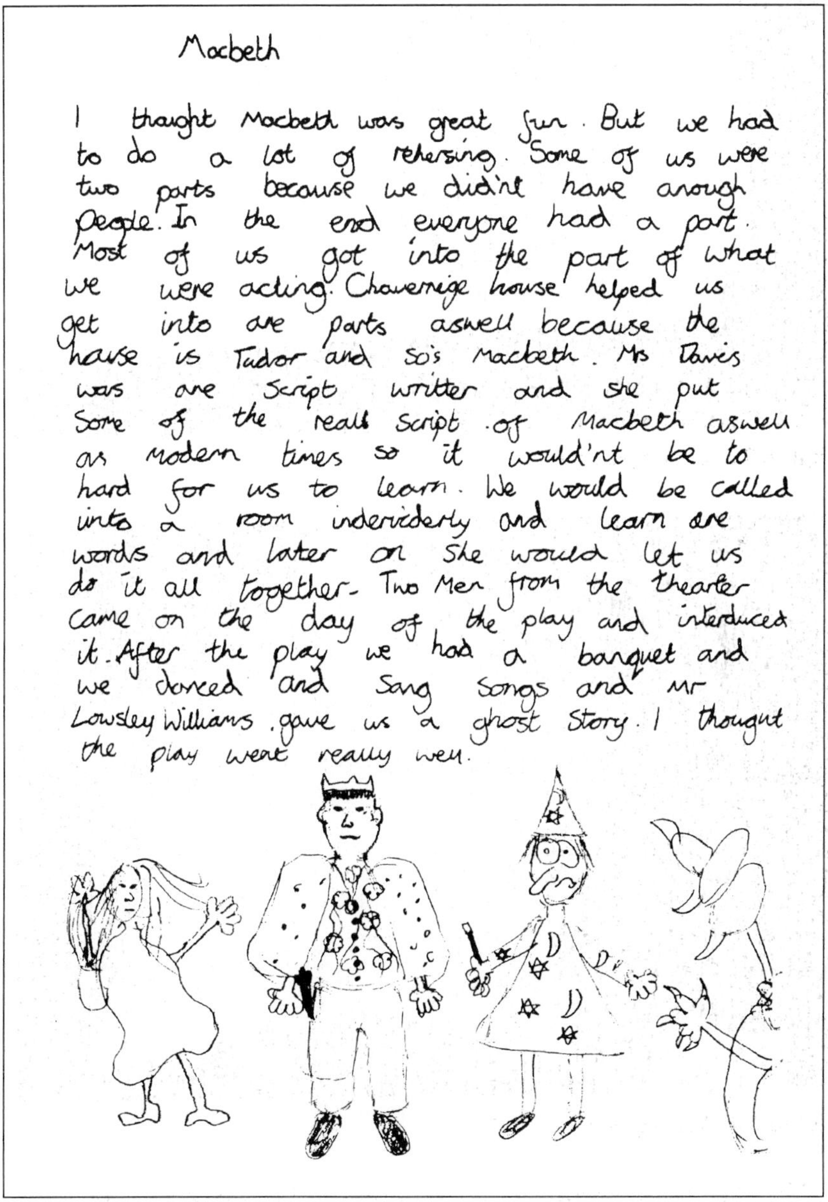

Figure 3.10 Reflections on *Macbeth*

Mapping the pattern or sequence of what took place

This is an activity which can encourage children to think through the sequence of what they did in their play. The children playing in the spaceship tried to sequence what they did through a series of pictures. Elizabeth took off in the spaceship, took the dog for a walk on the moon and returned to use the dog shower. She was able to talk about her play through her three pictures and provided her teacher with a good idea of her interests in her play. The children working on the Cabot play mapped out the pattern of their activities as they prepared for and produced the play.

Diaries of the way the play developed

One child involved in the *Macbeth* performance kept her own account of what occurred and her feelings as she participated in the play and it all came together. The first entry said:

> When we first knew we were going to do the play Macbeth I think we all felt a little bit of excitement. I thought at first we would have to research about Macbeth because we have not ever heard about Macbeth before. We didn't have to because we had the video and Judy told us the story of what it was all about.

The second entry:

> We were all very happy with our parts. I had two parts and my second part was a witch with Alice. My favourite bit in the play is when Macbeth and Lady Macbeth are arguing.

The third entry:

> We went to see C......... House and I know it is going to be a good night because it is a right atmosphere for the play with the balcony and everything.

The fourth entry:

> Today we have never stopped talking about the play. There were smiles and laughter all night. John and Mum and Dad really liked it. I was quite proud of myself because I didn't get anything muddled up and people said I was a good actress and I thought so too.

Although she wrote this for her own interest, it might be a strategy which could be incorporated in a drama activity to encourage children to begin to interpret and reflect on their own learning.

Summary

In this chapter we have considered ways in which teachers might collect information about children's responses in order to evaluate play activities. As we have already observed, not every episode of play is likely to be valuable, but in many of the examples we have described, children were given opportunities to communicate their sense-making within their play. In collecting evidence for summative assessments of children's learning there are many opportunities for teachers to add to what they know about children's responses in different curriculum areas. This evidence may be of a different kind from the information which emerges in subject specific activities. It can provide a window on how children are interpreting their activities and incorporating knowledge from different situations. Episodes of play draw from the complexities of the culture and the contexts in which they arise. Thus children not only demonstrate what they know within subject areas, but show how they make sense of their knowledge in wider cultural themes. In the next chapter we examine further ways of looking and understanding such episodes.

CHAPTER 4

Scripting Play: Exploring Narratives

Many of our examples of play so far have been associated with specific themes or topics. We have argued that these can provide contexts for free-flow play and opportunities for children to develop their understandings of the areas involved. We now want to look in detail at the mechanisms through which this can happen in order to justify further the presence of imaginative play in primary classrooms.

As we have already suggested, children begin to organise their knowledge about the world and predict interpretations and relationships based on events and experiences which emerge in their culture. In her book *The God of Small Things*, Arundhati Roy (1997) describes the arrival of eight-year-old Sophie Mol at the airport in India, where she meets her seven-year-old twin cousins for the first time:

> 'D'you know how to sashay?' Sophie Mol wanted to know.
> 'No. We don't sashay in India,' Ambassador Estha said.
> 'Well in England we do,' Sophie Mol said. 'All the models do. On television. Look – it's easy.'
> And the three of them, led by Sophie Mol, sashayed across the airport car park, swaying like fashion models. Eagle flasks and Made-in-England go-go bags bumping around their hips.
> (Roy 1997, p. 152)

The culture put across through television and artefacts resulted in a form of play which could be common to cousins even from different continents.

In the following example the culture embedded in a television programme provides a different kind of framework, one which enables two children to create a discourse reflecting appropriate forms and presentations. A brother and sister were playing at cooking and were almost silent as they collected what they needed and began mixing ingredients together and adding items. As they were doing this Peter commented:

> apple with the parsley – a mixture. You get it all nice and squeezed, squeezing orange peel [he squeezes an orange] mixed up, squeezed [as he shakes up the bottle containing apple juice], mixed up, squeezed [parsley and lemon juice], mixed up, squeezed [continues to shake bottle above his head] until it gets rather liquidy then it goes in the freezer.

This eight-year-old boy may have seen a cookery programme on television that gave his language a form, but his own interpretations emerged as a 'script' of his own making as he added ingredients to the mixture and began to imagine what the consistency might be.

The construct of 'script' in discourse analysis is useful in giving a fuller explanation of how children make use of the linguistic frameworks they meet in their daily encounters. Scripts are 'general event representations' which occur within social contexts. They have been seen as valuable in describing the beginnings of social knowledge and as an explanation for the way in which children make use of appropriate inferences in their discourse and interactions (Shank and Ableson 1977; Nelson 1981; Higgins, Ruble and Hartup 1983; Light 1987; Dunn 1988; Cortazzi 1993).

Shank and Abelson (1977) illustrate a script through a restaurant example where the script assumes waiters or waitresses, menus, bills, food and so on. By being able to call up such 'script knowledge', individuals are able to make predictions and inferences and develop imaginative sequences. The script is therefore at a very basic level and is well grounded and specific.

Katherine Nelson (1981) found that when three- to eight-year-old children were asked to tell 'what happened when …?, for example using a familiar event such as going to the supermarket, they were able to describe each aspect of the script as it was part of their social lives. Thus the script can be seen as the first level of approximation to the real world. It would seem that children acquire this knowledge from their experiences and as a result of their social relationships and interactions. This is usually through participating in these events or as an onlooker within the social milieu in which they live; for example, although children may not be involved in paying for goods at the checkout in the supermarket, they observe it happening from their own point of view. Such common experiences provide a shared knowledge base. They also enable an individual to predict what is likely to take place in a situation and know a sequence of actions and interactions which could occur.

Studies of script-based dialogues suggest that there are three components of a conversational context which contribute to maintaining a dialogue: presence of objects, a shared topic, and shared script knowledge. In episodes where three- to five-year-old children played with physical objects, their conversations were action referenced, discontinuous and short lived. Where the play became centred on a theme, the script helped to structure their interactions and develop their talk over a longer period of time (Nelson and Seidman 1984).

Drawing on a script allows children an opportunity for developing their understandings within a framework which is familiar to them. The theme of the script gives them certain expectations of what action and what language might be possible.

CASE STUDY

The home area

Three children, Chris, Debbie and Eve, all aged 4, are playing in a home area. Chris has a wooden spoon and a mixing bowl and is pretending to stir the contents. He is standing by the cooker. Debbie is looking at a cookery book, while Eve is dressing her doll at one of the tables.

Chris:	I've made ice cream for you.
Debbie:	I'll eat it in a minute thank you.
Eve:	Did you read the label?
Chris:	The instructions.
Debbie:	Four ounces of bananas, four ounces of apples and nine ounces of potatoes.
Chris:	We just read it.

Chris establishes the theme or script for the play in the first sentence by indicating that he is preparing food. Although Debbie is doing something else, she responds within the frame of the script: 'I'll eat it in a minute thank you.' Eve also maintains this, but introduces another aspect by referring to the print she has seen on supermarket items: 'Did you read the label?' Chris seeks clarification and this is taken up in detail by Debbie. The theme is maintained and the children are able to move within it to explore the meaning of the printed material in their own way. The turn taking and follow up comes quite naturally as they remain within their script framework. Each child is responding within the theme and is also aware of the comments of the others so that the theme and the script are actually unifying their interactions.

It is likely that experiencing scripts enables children to make more sense of social situations through identifying appropriate language. Planning how to act and what to say are made much easier when there is a script available. For example, a nursery-aged child is asked: 'What are you going to say to Mary when you ask her for a turn on the bike?' Sorting out the response goes some way to developing effective social interaction. Similarly, eleven-year-olds about to go to their secondary school develop some of the scripts they might need on the first day for finding the right classroom or organising lunch. Older pupils simulating interview techniques for mock interviews are learning the scripts that are going to help them through important situations.

The use of a familiar script for primary-aged children is helpful in providing them with a context in which they can join in at their own level. Children engaged in the space game described in Chapters 2 and 3 played in small groups which included children with English as a second language. The use of a familiar script, which included deciding which planet they would go to or the countdown and so on, was helpful in enabling them gradually to participate through language as well as through actions.

B2/G2: 9.8.7.6.5.4.3.2.1. Lift off …
G1:   Here we go, here we go.
G2:   It's dark …
B2:   And cold. Lights on …
B1:   Let's go to Mars today.
G1:   Oh no, I want to walk on the moon.

Girl 2 had played with this group on several occasions but had not said anything until this episode where she felt confident enough to join in with the countdown and make a contribution. The shared and familiar form of the script was a bridge between solitary and collaborative play, providing a context in which she could gain confidence in trying out her language.

The strategies children use to negotiate with one another within their scripts are also important, as to sustain a conversational script exchange within play, the script has to be a shared one. If one partner suggests 'let's play at picnics' it is no good if the others do not share the experience or are not willing to participate in the script. Skilled players in the use of scripts are aware of two levels of meaning as they take on roles in their play. They are operating as writer-directors and also as actors. Children have to develop their discourse strategies in order to negotiate their positioning within the script framework. The joint creation of the script is more than just a signal that 'this is play', it is an introduction to the rules of the game. This may come through overt proposals to pretend, but can only occur if all the participants agree to take it up and have the experiential knowledge to draw from.

The ways in which children agree to participate are sometimes very sophisticated, as Valerie Walkerdine showed in the following example:

Nancy: Hello Diana. Let's watch telly.
Diana: I'm just tidying baby's bed up. You sit on that wooden chair.
            Here y'are ... Alright I'm working ... I can't watch telly.
Nancy: Mum. Can I watch telly Mum. (1982, p. 133)

In this sequence Diane very carefully positions herself in control in the role of the mother. Although the negotiation is not explicit, the opening metaphor calls up a discourse that both children can participate in, but Diana plays it in the way she wishes it to be. Such a discourse will only continue if the participants have knowledge of the kinds of discourse their roles engender and continue to use the roles they have developed for themselves.

Scripting and development

Scripting is an important part of children's development as by experiencing sequences of interactions which are generalisable, they are learning about predictable forms of relationships. Paul Light stresses that 'much social knowledge may be implicit in scripted interaction without the child yet having appropriated that knowledge for himself' (1987, p. 56). This seems an important point to remember, particularly in play sequences where children may be trying out what they have seen and heard without really understanding what the interactions may mean. Because the discourse is extended across several turns children may appear to have a greater understanding than they actually have.

When this aspect of scripting is considered from another viewpoint, that of Vygotsky's 'zone of proximal development', we can see that it provides a useful context in which children may be showing what they think they know and how something may look to them. If we examine episodes where scripting may take place we are seeing developments very much from a child's viewpoint.

A study of three- to ten-year-old children playing together in groups of three to five showed that there was a clear developmental progression in moving into a fictional script (Auwarter 1986). It was found that older children had a structurally different mode of constructing the context by jumping immediately to the fictional level without any prepared steps. In the following extract a group of eight-year-olds show how they move immediately into their version of the story. They are playing with a storyboard which they have made based on *The Wind in the Willows*. Storyboards can be produced on thick card and can show the background layout for a story. In the *The Wind in the Willows* project children produced boards with a river running through, the wild woods and fields. They made miniature characters and some-times trees and houses so that they could move them around to represent parts of the story. The children in this episode had made their boards in groups and had discussed what they would need and where areas might be represented. As a result they were able to immediately move into their script.

They had set up the board showing Rat and Mole in their boat on the river and the picnic area complete with hamper and Toad and Badger strolling towards it from different directions. Using the different figures the children went into appropriate dialogues:

Mole: Oh, Oh, I am so excited. It is such a perfect day.
Rat: Pull the boat to the bank please my little velvet friend or we will never get to our picnic.
Toad: What can I see? What can I see? Food!
Badger: I smell something good. Maybe they will let me have some.

The story and the storyboard provided the script context into which all the children were able to move without difficulty and without planning what might happen beforehand.

Once dialogue is organised around shared script knowledge, children are able to reveal a high level of competence in exchanging information and keeping a conversation on target. The conversations between children when they are using shared script knowledge may well be characterised as true dialogues as they are often able to maintain coherence across many turns. Children frequently maintain the discourse of their script through repeating the theme and content of one another's talk. One partner might develop an idea and the other repeats it, or one might prompt another within the particular script framework (see the following case study).

In classrooms we provide children with a wide variety of scripts ranging from assemblies to responses to scientific experiments. Sometimes, a ready-made script such as the text of a story can enable children to play with their own knowledge.

CASE STUDY

The Very Hungry Caterpillar

Three children are in their second week of formal schooling. They are looking at the well-known children's story book *The Very Hungry Caterpillar*. The script arises from the theme of the book.

Alice: How – we have been talking about – bout caterpillars.
James: I've got that book.
Alice: And I have – there's holes in them – there's holes in the book ...
James: Yes – what's it about?
Alice: Caterpillar.

James: How can you read it 'cause I don't know how to read it – *[turning the pages]* he eated and eated and eated and eated and eated and eated and eated …

Alice: That night he had a stomach ache – and the next morning he through one nice fresh leaf – and he made – and he made – and he was so fat he made himself into a – made hiself …

Claire: Into a chrysalis.

Alice: Into a round thing called a chrysalis and the next morning he turned into a pretty butterfly.

Claire: No …

Alice: He nibbled through his chrysalis – and then out he came a beautiful butterfly but that is part of caterpillar but it's grown them and made wings you see.

Claire: And they wet.

In this episode the children are reflecting knowledge they have learnt in a different kind of classroom context where they have looked at a chrysalis and observed a butterfly emerging from it. Although they cannot read every word of the book they are familiar with the story and know some of the text. It therefore provides them with a script in which they can also explore their factual knowledge. All the way through the episode the children use the book script to help one another sort out what they know from their different experiences of caterpillars. An interjection by Claire – 'Into a chrysalis' – encourages Alice to reveal more of her knowledge and articulate it.

Alice: Into a round thing called a chrysalis and the next morning he turned into a pretty butterfly.

Claire: No …

Alice: He nibbled through his chrysalis – and then out he came a beautiful butterfly …

By supplying the appropriate term 'chrysalis', Claire helps Alice to use what she knows of the factual information and to remember parts of the story, making the connections as she does so. While not all books are going to enable children to generate a script and expand their understandings, it is worth noting the power of the picture book in encouraging children to develop their own conversations. They are immediately into a script which is meaningful and shared by all and can enable them to take forward their ideas.

Children are also able to move back and forth within their scripts to set up or explain the action, as when Alice says, 'How – we have been talking about – bout caterpillars' and James says, 'I've got that book'.

In another example, Carol Fox drew on her story data of 200 orally narrated stories by five children between the ages of three and six, to discuss Sundari's stories. In her narratives, Sundari is able to move in and out of her story all the time to make it clearer for the audience: 'and their houses – I might have told you them but I think I've forgotten – were called coggly woggly wogs', and later in the same story: 'and they have houses shaped like a diamond (P) with (P) triangle windows and square doors not oblong ones like you do have square ones' (1993, pp. 158–9).

Fox later points out that 'Children in their pretend play move in and out of role all the time. When they break the play and move out of role it is often to plan and set up the conditions for the next part of the act.' (1996, p. 62)

We now consider two case studies of the way in which classroom themes can provide children with a range of opportunities for developing scripts through their imaginative play. Both are based on book texts which have been used by the class as the basis for activities across curriculum. The first example is in a reception class and the second is in a class of eight-year-olds.

CASE STUDY

Mr Grinling. Do you know about him?

This was the question five-year-old Anwar asked a visitor to his classroom. He and his class had been involved in a topic based on the various adventures of the Lighthouse Keeper by Ronda and David Armitage from the Picture Puffin series: *The Lighthouse Keeper's Lunch*; *The Lighthouse Keeper's Catastrophe*; *The Lighthouse Keeper's Rescue*.

The classroom had been set up to include a climbing frame decorated to represent a lighthouse (Figure 4.1). There were various ropes going from it to the home area and a pulley system which enabled children to send a basket with letters and various foods along the rope between the lighthouse and the lighthouse keeper's cottage (Figure 4.2).

The children had made friezes and drawn and written about the stories. There was a concept keyboard overlay which included names and the more difficult words. There was also a language master and a further set of words for children to identify and use in their writing. The following activities occurred during the four weeks of the project.

1. One morning the children made sandwiches to tempt the seagulls. These included different kinds of jam, peanut butter, banana, marmite, meat and fish pastes. They then recorded which kind they themselves preferred and made a chart of this.
2. The teacher produced a box of keys for the children to experiment with to try to find the one which fitted the treasure chest.
3. On another morning the teacher invested in two fish from the fishmonger for the children to feel, touch, smell and draw and also comment on as they began to be less than fresh.

Figure 4.1 The lighthouse   **Figure 4.2** The pulley system

These activities provided a rich background for the dramatic and socio-dramatic play which occurred when the children chose to be in the role-play area. Anwar had been trying to explain the episode in *The Lighthouse Keeper's Catastrophe* when Mr Grinling had shut the cat Hamish in the lighthouse with the key also inside. He tried to climb in through the window but was too fat to get in. This appealed to the children, as Anwar's version showed: 'When the … He locked him in the door. Then he tried to go through the window and he got stuck. Mr Grinling. Do you know about him? Michelle's gone to get the book.'

The book was seen as giving a fuller explanation and carried the pictures which the children all enjoyed and which helped them to explain the story.

Each day the class reviewed what had taken place. They were able to say what they had been doing in the lighthouse, in the cottage and also comment on their role play. One day Jane took on the role of Mrs Grinling. When asked what had happened she said:

Jane: Mr Grinling came in for his tea.
Teacher: How did he come in?
Jane: He stomped in in his big boots.
Teacher: Did he say anything?
Jane: He said, where is the tea? All gruff he was.

David, who was Mr Grinling, had got a real feel for his role largely from the pictures in the books and his wellington boots. He had also put his character across to Jane. When the two acted out this episode they were able to add to the language and pick up even more of the dialogue from the story.

On another occasion two boys were engaged in problem solving. They spent most of the afternoon trying out an assortment of keys to see which one fitted a small chest. The children had written labels on the keys as in the story *The Lighthouse Keeper's Catastrophe*. The keys were all of different sizes and there were many to try. The following morning the two boys rushed into the classroom and began trying the keys again. They would not leave their task, even for registration. Finally having decided to sort the keys into large and small and worked through the groups systematically, they approached their teacher:

Peter: Mrs M the key is not there.
Mrs M: Are you sure? Have you tried all of them?
Peter: Yes all of them.
Mrs M: Try this one then.

She produced another key from a string around her neck. The boys were extremely angry and disgusted. An injustice had been done.

Peter: That is cheating. You had it all the time.

Fortunately they were allowed to open the chest. Nevertheless, their indignation took a while to subside. In spite of their good relationship with their teacher she did go down in their estimations for a while. What was very apparent was their perseverance, which had gone way beyond any time spent on other activities, and their problem solving skills were more than challenged. At review time they told the others what had taken place and were still so indignant that Ms M felt she had to apologise, again a good lesson for the children.

In another example from review time, David asked the question, 'Why couldn't Mr Grinling get through the window?' After looking at the pictures very carefully, Alice and Eleanor both had answers:

Alice: He was too fat.
Eleanor: The window was too small.

This resulted in further discussion by the group as to which was the best explanation and why, and further reference to the pictures. David (Mr Grinling) and Eleanor (Mrs Grinling) then did their own dramatic representation of what took place:

David: I can get in through the window I think.
Eleanor: Go on then, up the ladder.
David: Oh dear it is high. I feel dizzy.
Eleanor: Oh go on, be brave and don't look down.
David: I can see Hamish but I can't get through, the window is too small.
Eleanor: Let me pull your heavy trousers to get you back.

The language of the story provided extra support for the children which they were able to use as a script for their role play.

After several days of free-play we noticed that it was always the boys climbing the lighthouse and tending the light, as did Mr Grinling in the story. The girls looked after the home area in the lower part of the lighthouse, or were in the cottage (home area) back on shore. On one occasion two girls were on a small boat on the waves and needed rescuing – again by the boys. At one of the small group review times it just happened that there were seven girls in the group and no boys. The conversation turned to gender issues when one child noticed this:

Rheanna: There are only girls in this group.
Arifa: It's better.
Teacher: Why?
Girls: Boys are a nuisance. They push you out. They don't know it all.
Teacher: Would you rather do all your work in a girls' group or in a group with some boys?
Arifa: Just girls.
Rheanna: Yeah, girls are better.

The teacher decided to manipulate the play a little and one morning only the girls played in the area while the boys chose other things. This was unusual as the children did follow a plan, do, review, system based on the High/Scope model for the two sessions in the morning and during the afternoon. There were activities related to the basic skills which they had to do during the day, but they were able to choose where until that area was filled. The girls were a little surprised and did very little climbing of the lighthouse. One girl, Maria, spent a great deal of time with one of the ropes tying it to a chair and working on tensions. She did this on her own and concentrated for around 20 minutes. Other children did their usual activities and sent letters, messages and food to the lighthouse.

Although they enjoyed their activities without the boys, the nature of their play was not so very different from when they played with them. Murphy and Elwood (1997) suggest that in school situations, boys are 'more likely to tackle tasks with confidence if they believe it is in their "territory"'. Both girls and boys are likely to see different aspects of what they observe in a task as significant. This was particularly the case in the play episodes in this classroom where the boys were involved in making the pulley work while the girls wrote notes to go in the basket. Seeing Maria working with the ropes, which she had not done before, was a good reason for occasionally manipulating the play so that all children had a chance to try out different aspects of the activities and experiment as they wished.

We have described this example very fully because it shows the way in which the free play activities were incorporated into the planning of the work of this class over several weeks. Although the actual area was structured to represent the lighthouse and the cottage, the way the children played in it was entirely their own. Each episode of the story involved different activities which were included among the props or added to the writing or art opportunities, and on several occasions children developed their own imaginative scripts based on the story.

Several curriculum areas were developed through the activities generated by the theme.

English:
- speaking and listening skills in repeating and sequencing the stories;
- acting out different episodes;
- writing stories drawing on the books and vocabulary;
- own reading of the books;
- confirming details from the books;
- suggesting descriptive words for the fish.

Mathematics:
- sorting keys according to size and shape;
- weighing and balancing using the pulley;
- graphing different kinds of sandwiches
- counting different kinds of fish.

Science:
- different ingredients for sandwiches and noting whether tastes were sweet or savoury;
- touching and smelling fish and noting changes in their condition over time.

Art:
- drawings for the frieze;
- detailed drawings of the fish using different crayons, pencils, chalks and paints.

DT:
- setting up and using the ropes and pulley.

IT:
- using the concept keyboard to create stories.

In the planning for this unit of work, which occurred over one half term, the teacher involved had looked at the balance of the curriculum and taken account of the areas of learning for four-year-olds and subject content at Key Stage 1. What then emerged was as a result of the children's interpretations of their activities and the opportunities for play which were available to them.

CASE STUDY

Let's all eat scrap metal

In this example a Year 3 class had read the story of *The Iron Man* by Ted Hughes, a compelling story which appeals to the imagination. It includes both drama and empathy and has been a popular text in many primary classrooms since its publication in 1966. The book was used as part of a topic on Materials, but swiftly took off in the children's imaginative activities. Early on in the project it had been decided to create a scrap-metal dump with samples and examples and pictures collected by the class. After a visit to a rubbish dump where the materials were categorised according to materials and size of objects, the children noted the categories such as old cars and lorries in one area; cookers, fridges in another, and old prams, carts and bikes in another. They were fascinated by this and designed their rubbish dumps on storyboards so that articles could be moved around. Models of the Iron Man were also made so that different scenarios could be played out. It was decided to have one area of the classroom as a radio station in order to enact different aspects of the story. Groups of children chose their own events in the story and acted them out, recording them if they wished. Episodes emerged such as:

- Hoggarth first seeing the Iron Man;
- preparing the trap;
- the Iron Man in the scrap yard;
- being an eye. (One child had been to Disneyworld in Florida and had been impressed by an exhibit at the EPCOT Centre where parts of the human body gave instructions to their owner on how they should be treated.)

Some writing occurred in planning these episodes but on the whole they were part of the role play in the radio station.

More structured activities such as prose and poetry writing were also included in classroom activities. The text of the story lent itself to language which was easily remembered and repeatable and children were keen to take this on board: 'The Iron Man came to the top of the cliff. How far had he walked? Nobody knows. Where had he come from? Nobody knows. How was he made? Nobody knows' (Hughes 1986, p. 11).

This led to many versions based on different scenarios within the book and in the rubbish dump. Simon and Mike recorded the following script from the radio station:

Simon: The saucepans were piled up in a great heap. They were higher than a boy, higher than a man. They were higher than the church.
Mike: Where had they come from? Nobody knows. Where were they made? Nobody knows. What had they cooked? Nobody knows.

They then began to play with the theme and their imaginative ideas began to flow:

Simon: But one of the saucepans still has some food in it. Look, dried up spaghetti and snails.
Mike: This one had horrible spinach and carrots. Why didn't anyone eat it? Nobody, nobody, nobody knows.

This playing with words was very popular and occurred in many of the recordings. The teacher found that she sometimes needed to introduce new ideas to encourage variety in the episodes which emerged. A discussion and debate on the moral dilemmas involved in the story resulted in a different kind of episode for recording based on the Iron Man's decision to go to Australia and challenge the space-bat-angel-dragon. Two children argued about whether the Iron Man should go when he could easily break up into pieces. The boy taking the role of the Iron Man was not keen to go: 'No I am only as big as a tall tree, I am not big enough. Besides I like it here eating these old gas stoves.' He was eventually persuaded by another child playing Hoggarth: 'Please go and save the world, after all there will be no food in scrap yards if you don't.' The play episodes were also of a different nature to those of the infant age groups. The junior children were keen to prepare a more finished episode for recording, even though their initial activities were often in the play mode.

This carries important implications for the kinds of play experiences we provide for children. If we do wish to encourage imaginative play and enable children to develop their strengths in language, then the role-play themes are important to support and extend their use of vocabulary and presentation. By encouraging play to occur we are also providing opportunities for children to share their understandings and make sense of some of the aspects of their learning which need further exploration.

Summary

In this chapter we have considered the possibilities a script can offer in analysing the discourses and actions children engage in when they play. It would seem that as a way of looking at what children do when they are playing, scripting can reveal some of the processes through which children try to make sense of their social experiences. Examples of play scripts and case studies of different age groups have been discussed to demonstrate links in conversational inferences which relate to overall themes. The chapter emphasises that scripting in play episodes is a means through which children's thinking and interactions can be reflected and observed.

CHAPTER 5

Play at the Core: Exploring Literacy and Numeracy

In this book we are concerned to show the different kinds of information which can be gained through observing children in episodes of classroom play. We now focus on the ways in which children's knowledge of literacy and numeracy may be extended through their play experiences. The question is raised as to which aspects of learning in these core subjects can only be demonstrated and will only arise when they are part of the play function.

Throughout this book the notion of pretend play in encouraging imaginative ideas and interpretations has been stressed. We have also acknowledged that, in practice, play is often given low priority in the curriculum and pedagogy of the primary school; it could be and often is sidelined in favour of the teaching of the basic skills. However, where play is integral to the planning of curriculum activities it provides opportunities for children to demonstrate significant and ongoing understandings. Returning to our original model, we suggest that the language and operations of literacy and numeracy can be practised and tried out in play. These discourses can incorporate subject knowledge and also reflect the cultural experiences in which children have encountered written symbols in use (see Figure 5.1).

One of us has recently acquired new literacy and numeracy knowledge through the culture of the supermarket. No longer do we buy our purchases willy nilly, not really noting what things cost in our rush to get out the other end; instead we hold a handset which enables us to tag each item so that by the time we reach

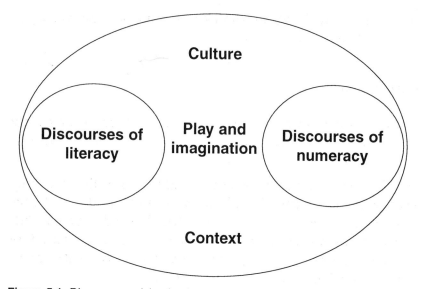

Figure 5.1 Discourses arising in play

the cash desk we have an itemised bill and we have packed our own shopping on the way round. We see very young children also involved in this process, often trying to do it too. There are young children who cannot yet read looking very carefully at the markings and prices for each item before their parents let them use the handset to tag what has been bought. This is a particular way of using literacy and numeracy which will probably, of course, have changed by the time they become parents, but at the moment parents and children are learning to use a set of symbols and behaviours which are characteristic of that supermarket context.

As children gain specific knowledge of the contexts in which both literacy and numeracy occur, they like to practice the actions they have seen carried out, often showing what they have observed of the purposes of symbols in their environment. Some schools and classrooms have play areas which provide opportunities for children to try out reading and writing and numeracy in natural settings and demonstrate their understandings of the contexts in which they have experienced symbols of print.

As we explore each area in detail we show how imaginative role play can be part of long- and short-term curriculum planning and assessment. The main issue to be considered is what more we can learn about children's knowledge of literacy and numeracy through their play activities.

Literacy worlds

> We have to learn to read not just words, texts or even a variety of discourses but the contexts and conventions of how the discourses work. (Meek 1991, p. 35)

The discourses related to what we might call functional literacy arise from knowledge about how print works in different contexts. Research over the last 20 years has shown that young children have many experiences of print and the way it is used before they enter formal schooling (Ferreiro and Teberoski 1983; Heath 1983; Harste, Woodward and Burke 1984).

Anderson and Stokes call these experiences 'literacy events', which denote 'any action sequence involving one or more persons in which the production or comprehension of print plays a significant role' (1984, p. 26). These events occur as part of the flow of everyday life. Sometimes they are focused for children, as when adults involve them in specific activities such as signing and drawing on a birthday card, or they occur on the margins of awareness as children are engaging in their own activities. An example of this is when parents and children are at a bank or post office where reading and writing may be going on; children are not involved but may be subconsciously aware of the specific activities to do with print which are taking place. Seeing notices read, cheques written, forms signed, money or stamps passed across a counter are all part of the flow of literacy events which are part of their daily experience.

There is no doubt that where a play area is enriched by print, children will experiment with mark making and writing. Examples of children engaged in literacy activities as part of their play in nursery and infant class contexts have been documented by Hall (1987), Hall and Abbott (1991), Christie (1991), Neuman and Roskos (1992), Moyles (1994) and Hall and Robinson (1995). What these studies have shown is that play can be a productive context for reflecting children's literacy understandings.

Play areas using print in early years classrooms

The notion of a play area which includes print materials was first developed by Hall (1987). An example was a 'literate home corner', where paper, pencils, newspapers, planners, telephone directories, cookery books and catalogues were all added as part of the environment. Hall's study, in which a home corner was subjected to this 'print flood' showed that during four days children were engaged in 290 literacy events in conjunction with their dramatisations. These included, for example, checking through catalogues for items to buy and looking at newspapers for TV programmes. Later work by Hall and Abbott (1991) and Hall and Robinson (1995) shows the kinds of writing experiences which teachers may encourage through providing appropriate contexts and materials.

Hall and Abbott (1991) maintain that play based on real-life experiences offers children valuable opportunities to experiment explicitly with reading and writing and demonstrate what they know of the symbols of their culture. They identify four levels of specificity which emerge in literacy activities associated with play:

1. physical exploration of resources;
2. symbolic play associated with specific kinds of symbolic behaviour, e.g. mark making as writing;
3. play involving a certain explicitness in language;
4. children being literate people.

The physical environment of the classroom and the way this is organised to promote literacy opportunities has been shown to be an important element in informal literacy learning. An extensive study by Neuman and Roskos (1992) explored whether play settings enriched with literacy objects influenced the frequency and complexity of literacy demonstrations by pre-schoolers. The study took place over a seven-month period in two pre-school settings with 91 three- to five-year-olds. Neuman and Roskos intervened in one setting by adding reading and writing materials in all play areas. They found that the frequency, duration and complexity of children's play with print increased and that the objects encouraged self-generated literacy activity. A particularly interesting finding was that children in the intervention group often transformed the literacy objects into something else, for example the cook books became magic genie books as agreed by all the children.

Neuman and Roskos (1992) also identify some limitations. They suggest that although these print-enriched environments encouraged literacy-related play, it was not clear whether this had any meaning for the children in their classroom learning. As they say: 'the utility of these objects in building up stores of represented meanings to be used at some later time in more abstract forms of literacy use may be limited' (p. 221).

This question of how far demonstrations of literacy-related play carry a wider meaning for the children is an important one. While young children may demonstrate their use of print materials and their purposes, they may not be relating this to the symbolic representations of print that they meet as part of their school culture. It seems important that we should always be thinking of how play experiences can be incorporated into the overall planning for the class so that connections can be made.

In a case study of 'the garage' (Hall and Robinson 1995), connections with writing were made throughout the play activities. After a visit to a local garage, four- and five-year-old children and their teachers decided to build a garage as a play area. This required getting planning permission, filling out forms, drawing up plans and arranging a grand opening. Many writing activities occurred in which the children took part with enthusiasm, understanding the purposes for their writing and appreciating many complex writing events such as making complaints or writing invitations. Although these children were beginning writers they took an intense interest in the writing they were engaged in because they had a 'powerful sense of audience' and knew the different people their writing was for. As Hall and Robinson (1995) point out, this was a classroom where play was regarded as important and included as part of the overall planning for the activities of the class.

The success of the above project was also due to the many discussions which took place with children in making decisions about the play area and what writing needed to be done. This meant that all the play was part of ongoing classroom activities and never divorced from them, thus enabling children to make connections about the uses of print in a realistic situation.

In looking at the way in which children's writing may develop it is also important to note what play may offer as children begin to gain mastery of their writing. There is a point in writing development where children are concerned to get their letters and words correct. The early writing which emerges from children may look like marks on paper and may represent a story, but children soon begin to appreciate that there is a correct way to write letters and are keen to do so. Questions such as 'Is this how you write Donna?' are part of this keenness to get it right. In play children are able to experiment and also request help.

In their work on the 'child as informant' Harste *et al.* (1984, p. 156) give an example of Zac, aged six, who attempted to be correct and practise the same writing examples on several occasions. Zac spent each day in a play area set up as an airport. On the first day he made drawings of planes taking off, on another day he gave them names and tried to show where they were going, while on another day he sat in the office area and wrote his report about a plane crashing.

Although his writing attempts and spelling were not perfect he was gaining confidence in his ability to represent meanings through the symbol systems of writing. He was also doing this in his own way and in his own time so that he was in control of his own learning throughout his play episodes.

In another example, Philip, aged seven, wrote about looking after your child as a pet. He did this on a daily basis, adding to it when he felt the need and sometimes in between playing with his pet rabbit (Figure 5.2).

Such writing is often part of the ongoing play taking place and may be very rough. Teachers may wish to add children's informal writing to their records as it provides evidence which is very personal to children's own meanings and wishes. It often includes use of the structure, spelling and punctuation which they have acquired in other writing experiences in the classroom.

The support which teachers are able to give to this early writing is important in providing children with models of how it might go. Making large books with children where teachers model the writing of children's versions of their experiences or a

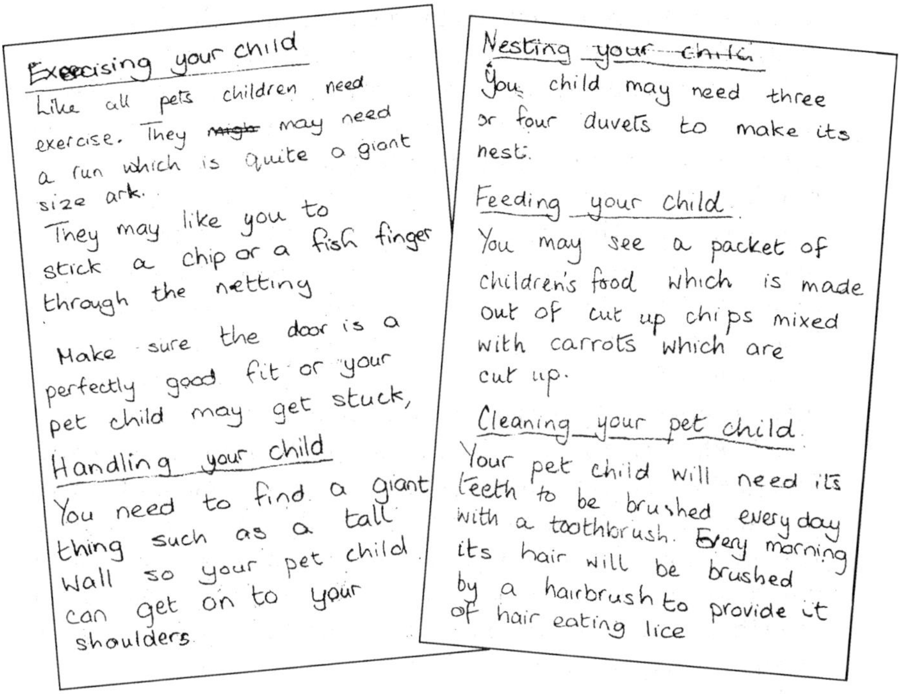

Exercising your child

Like all pets children need exercise. They migh may need a run which is quite a giant size ark.

They may like you to stick a chip or a fish finger through the netting

Make sure the door is a perfectly good fit or your pet child may get stuck,

Handling your child

You need to find a giant tall thing such as a wall so your pet child can get on to your shoulders.

Nesting your child

You child may need three or four duvets to make its nest.

Feeding your child.

You may see a packet of children's food which is made out of cut up chips mixed with carrots which are cut up.

Cleaning your pet child.

Your pet child will need its teeth to be brushed every day with a toothbrush. Every morning its hair will be brushed by a hairbrush to provide it of hair eating lice

Figure 5.2 Your child as a pet

familiar story provide the model for confident attempts at early writing. In the work on the Lighthouse Keeper stories (see Chapter 4), children did their own writing using the vocabulary available to them from the books. This was produced on cards for their own Breakthrough to Literacy (1972) folders and on a Language Master. They had also made big books where their teacher had scribed the texts, for example *Sandwiches for Mr Grinling*. When children were sending packages and messages for Mr Grinling in the basket from the cottage to the lighthouse, they took great delight in making labels and writing notes in a confident way, so practising their writing skills.

Conversations which occur in play are significant in contributing to children's sense-making processes. As has already been shown, the scripts which children use provide them with opportunities to collaborate in understanding the topics and concepts which are part of their classroom learning. This notion is supported by the work of Neuman and Roskos who showed that conversations around literacy were part of the flow of the children's play and approximated to a 'collaborative learning model' (1992, p. 221). Partners served complementary roles, sometimes helping one another and sometimes engaging in disagreements. Neuman and Roskos argued that many of these conversations included designating and labelling written objects, for example:

A: Look this is a dinosaur right? … So is this right?

S: That isn't a pterodactyl. It doesn't have wings.

The children's conversations also included negotiation to establish shared meaning and coaching to teach or guide each other's learning.

The findings of Neuman and Roskos were reiterated by Vukelich (1993) who argued that in peer activities involving writing, play should be recognised as a form of thought and is crucial in our understanding of how children can and do learn. She used four settings in which 231 peer writing-related activities were observed – a restaurant, a shoe store, a veterinary hospital and a campsite – and found that children provided three kinds of writing information to one another during their play.

1. Writing to provide information about the functions of writing, such as:
    - writing to help others remember, e.g. a food order, recording appointments or a prescription;
    - writing to share what you know with others;
    - writing to control others' behaviour;
    - writing to announce events;
    - writing to get things done or help others.

2. Providing information about the features of print, e.g. how do you make an 'r'.

3. Providing information about the meaning of print. To use an example from the campsite, three children, aged five, were looking at a sign written by a forest ranger. It said: 'RAKNS R IN KMP' (Raccoons are in camp):

    S: What do you think this sign says?

    J: Too many people in camp?

    S: No I don't think so.

    K: What does the sign say?

S: Hmm, it says, um what do you think?

K: I can't read yet. You can read. What does it say?

The meaning of the sign is never determined.

Vukelich concludes: 'These descriptions do suggest that play with peers in literacy-enriched settings provides the conditions for young children to interact about the functions, features and meaning of their writing, and these interactions provide the potential for learning to occur' (1993, p. 391). This is where the review times can be particularly important in enabling children to recall and reflect on their activities. In reviewing children's understandings of literacy as it emerges in their play, we can see that play episodes provide opportunities for them to use their knowledge from different contexts in which print is used. This can be extended through the support of the classroom environment and teachers building on what is taking place.

Literacy demonstrations in primary classroom settings

The ways in which junior-aged children make sense of literacy also emerge in the off-task interactions and conversations which occur around activities in the classroom. Playing with talk can be valuable in encouraging children's thinking as Dyson (1989) found in her studies of eight-year-old children's discussions about the themes of their writing. Drawing upon the ideas of Bruner, Halliday (1975) and Vygotsky, Dyson showed that verbal interactions about written language were an important support for children in helping them to construct the way their writing might develop. Her analysis of the off-task collaboration and spontaneous conversations which took place between children as they engaged in classroom writing activities showed that this enabled them to critique and extend their story writing. By gathering descriptive data from eight children of different ethnic and social backgrounds, Dyson identified certain categories in the exchanges which took place. These were:

1. collaborative reflections on possible worlds;
2. providing the characters of imaginary worlds;
3. analysing and critiquing possible worlds;
4. anticipating audience reaction.

These categories were apparent in a class of eight-year-olds where three children were creating a story on the word processor arising from their theme play in connection with the ocean liner (see Chapter 2). Three children had decided to let the liner take them to a country with a desert. They had decided what they would take and were now developing a description and adventure that happened while they were there. Their discussion included several of the categories identified by Dyson.

Jane: It's no good putting in that they grew vegetables like potatoes because we don't know in the desert. (Category 1)

Stephen: I think they have dates from palm trees so we could put that in. (1)

Ann: And prickly pear but I'm not sure you can eat it.

Stephen: Shall we have a traveller? (2)

Jane: You mean like a Samaritan? (2)

Stephen: Well he could carry water and then if he meets someone in the desert he could help them. (2)

Ann: Yes, let's put that in.

Jane: Is a Samaritan in this desert though? I thought he was in Palestine. (3)

Ann: Yes, it must be the same desert. (3)

Stephen: Well there is nothing exciting yet and they won't read it if we don't make it more interesting. (4)

The children then went on to reorganise the text.

Ann: We could say, The desert was hot and dry and full of yellow sand and stones. There was nothing to eat or drink for miles and miles. The children were very tired when along came an rocket with yellow and black stripes.

Stephen: They shouted and waved their arms but it flew over and round them. Then it threw out a big bundle with a tent.

Jane: And a camel came parachuting down and a space man.

Dyson argues that by being given the opportunity to talk with one another about their writing, children are able to reflect and manipulate their ideas through spontaneous interaction. The most elaborate verbal stories and manipulations of narrative occurred in the children's talk rather than in their writing as they discussed what might happen and the characters involved. The play aspect of the activities gave children valuable opportunities for extending their ideas.

Encouraging children to compose texts in pairs or groups is a way of enabling them to share and play with the content and vocabulary of their writing. In both the ocean liner and recording studio themes (see Chapter 2), the collaboration gave children freedom to set about the tasks as they wished. Where they were encouraged to talk to one another about their stories, they could focus on the plots, characters, dialogue, spelling and punctuation and gain confidence in revising their ideas. The following example shows how a second group of children in the ocean liner role-play area moved in and out of reality as they played with ideas for their story.

Susanne: We could make these people very rich.
Claire:　　How about a weekend in Rome darling?
Susanne: (Posh voice) I don't have a thing to wear.
Claire:　　Buy some silk dresses when we get there.
Susanne: Shall we get a plane off the ship and go today?
Claire:　　Could you do that or would it be a helicopter?

Playing with words and with the subject matter all emerged in the collaborative play of children in these role-play areas and was evident in their final pieces of written language.

What emerges from this example and from Dyson's work is the importance of examining the particular discourses which occur in episodes of play in which literacy is a part. We can not only gain a greater understanding of how children are making sense of the task but also begin to identify the distinctive features of how they are interpreting and extending their knowledge of the structures and different genres of written language. We should also acknowledge the additional support which teachers give in providing stories, poetry and informative material to encourage ideas which can be taken further in the play. The activities for the ocean liner and the recording studio were carefully planned and extended as the play took off to make the most of opportunities for play and thinking to occur.

Literacy as reflected in dramatic play

Play which is focused on a story gives children opportunities to try out literary texts as well as develop their play along the lines of a particular theme. Christie (1991) argues cogently for the value of print as an integral part of dramatic play in the classroom. He maintains that it provides children with the opportunity not only to 'experiment with writing, spelling and reading in rich contextualised situations and specific settings', but also to 'engage in dramatic play which can help to develop their knowledge of a story structure by having the opportunity to invent and act out their own narratives' (Christie 1991, p. 36).

In play episodes children's language often emerges from the styles and discourses of the texts which they have experienced or read. Carol Fox (1993) found that children between the ages of three and six could tell oral stories using the language of the books they knew even before they were able to read. If this is the case then we should do our best to provide the kinds of settings which can encourage children to demonstrate their knowledge of the language of the different genres included in the range of texts available to them.

Interactions between children in their imaginative play can be encouraged through specific teaching strategies. The use of puppet plays to encourage narrative strategies has been documented by Daniels (1994). In one example two six-year-olds based their play on *Supergran to the Rescue*. They also used the script for going shopping to develop aspects of the episode. The transcript revealed 'how central imaginative play is' (p. 120) in developing the functions of language as children participate in creating their own discourses within the framework of a story.

The National Curriculum Orders for English at Key Stages 1 and 2 (1995) and the National Literacy Strategy (1998) stress the range of texts which pupils should be encouraged to read. This includes poems and stories based on imaginary or fantasy worlds, folk tales and fairy stories, myths, legends and traditional stories, and texts from a variety of cultures and traditions: 'They should be introduced to a wide range of literature and have opportunities to read extensively for their own interest and pleasure and for information' (DfE 1995, p. 13).

This variety of material suggests many opportunities for children to experience and use the language of texts. This might occur through stimulating play episodes and encouraging children to extend language through basing their play on the discourses which emerge in the stories (see Chapter 4).

Summary of 'literacy worlds'

In this section we have explored the play opportunities which primary classrooms may offer children in supporting their knowledge of reading and writing. Such demonstrations can be valuable in showing children's functional knowledge of their experiences and sometimes their mistaken ideas about the information available to them. We now look at the ways some of these same play settings can provide opportunities for mathematical understandings to occur.

Mathematical worlds

Play that is personally meaningful for children in encouraging their thinking has much to offer as part of the mathematical curriculum. For young children there is a stress on mathematics occurring through practical activities, for example, in outcomes such as 'They recognise and use numbers to 10 and are familiar with larger numbers from their everyday lives' and 'They begin to use their developing mathematical understanding to solve practical problems' (SCAA 1996, p. 3). Similarly, at Key Stages 1 and 2, pupils should have opportunities to 'use and apply mathematics in practical tasks, in real life problems and within mathematics itself' and should be developing skills in 'devising and defining their own ways of recording' and 'handling data and solving problems' (DfE 1995, pp. 26–7).

Children of all ages often set themselves difficult challenges in their play and are likely to want to follow through many of their thematic investigations with the use of mathematical skills and knowledge (Griffiths 1994). Much that is learnt informally before entering school and outside school will often reveal itself in play as children construct their own understandings of mathematical situations. Teachers may encourage this by '(i) making mathematics the starting point and making sure mathematical experiences are planned for within the play; (ii) establishing play areas based on particular themes with the mathematical experiences emerging incidentally. We might term these second experiences "mathematical actions"' (Van Oers 1994, p. 2). Both approaches can emerge through creating role-play areas and each can offer children opportunities to develop their mathematical activities.

In an example of the first approach, Van Oers describes a shoe shop (1994, pp. 10–11). Over several sessions 'pupils spontaneously used notational means to indicate the respective classes of shoes; on other opportunities children started to make drawings of the classified and coded piles of shoes and indeed started to operate "mathematically" on these representations' (1994, p. 5).

He also describes an occasion where a teacher participated in the activities and was able to guide children to reflect upon the process taking place. The teacher is asking children for shoes that go together. Pupils are busy putting shoes on the shelves.

Teacher: Well, I think we have a problem here again. If someone wants to buy this shoe *(points to one shoe in the rack)* how are we gonna find the other one?

Pupils start opening boxes, looking for the matching shoe.

Teacher: That's a lot of work! Is there no way we can find to do this more quickly, finding the right shoe? We must be sure that we find the right shoe easily.
Pupil: We must leave the tops off the boxes.
Teacher: Yes, but then it is difficult to make piles. Maybe it's a good idea to make something for the outside of the box so that you can recognise what's inside?
Pupil: Yes I know! I know!
Teacher: Tell me what you are looking for.
Pupil: We gonna put letters on them.
Teacher: Which letters?

While the teacher is very involved in raising questions and encouraging the children to solve problems as part of their activity, one wonders how long it would have taken the children to solve some of these problems for themselves or by helping one another. There is certainly an argument for teachers using play to further children's conceptual understandings and the point of this particular episode was in highlighting the mathematical opportunities which the teacher could encourage through children's practical activities.

In an example quoted by Davis and Pettitt (1994, p. 14), a teacher introduces the idea of the 'silly milkman' to a group of five-year-olds playing with a Duplo lorry taking bottles of milk to different houses. The teacher finds herself in the role of the milkman and where a message asks for two pints of milk she leaves three. The children are perplexed until the teacher challenges them: 'I bet you can't make the silly milkman give you the milk you really want.' One child works this out: 'Caught you, silly milkman. I wanted two pints. That's why I said one pint!' They go on playing the game until the teachers suggests the next 'silly milkman' tries another rule. The play goes on with the children setting up new problems and trying to solve them. Davis points out that the teacher enabling rather than directly teaching does not always work out and can lead to frustration as when one child asked for 'no pints today please' and the rule of 'one too few' could not be resolved. Nevertheless, the dilemma led to much discussion by the children as they tried to work out why the rule did not help them.

Mathematics arising incidently in role-play areas

In the following case study the mathematical experiences emerge incidently as three children try to make sense of the symbols of print.

CASE STUDY

The train station

Christopher, Adam and Alex, all aged four, are in their first term in school and are playing in a role-play area set up as a train station. There is a ticket office with timetables, tickets, picture of trains and journeys and maps around for the children to look at. This provides opportunities for making and issuing tickets, preparing menus for the restaurant car and reading guidebooks and timetables. There are also areas for passengers to sit while they wait for the trains. This has emerged as part of a theme of Journeys for a mixed Reception and Year 1 class; the printed material is embedded in the activity of going on a journey and taking a train to get there. Although the teacher is not aware of this, the three boys are devotees of *Thomas the Tank Engine* and played train games on several occasions at their playgroup before entering the school (Beardsley 1988). When invited to play in the train station they begin by drawing upon this shared context, but are much more involved in making sense of the numbers.

Adam: You going on that train 10410? You have to hold on tight 'cause that will go really fast. You have to take your flask.
Alex: This is the one Sooty going on. It goes really fast like that.
Chris: It gets in at 1 o'clock.
Adam: You're going – that many – 10.
Chris: I want the struction book.
Alex: The London cars are on that one. On that one they are – the London cars.
Adam: The London cars should be on the motorway – er …
Alex: But they can go on – so you are on the London, right at the back. Right at the top nearly and the rest is right at the top.
Adam: The steam train goes – hang on. The steam goes that fast, it goes really fast like this.
Chris: Yes, that fast train I showed you. You can go to sleep on – 064907.
Alex: Hot dinners are put in.
Chris: Have I left the travel on?
Alex: Hot dinners. I've told the train men.
Chris: To go to there.
Alex: Yes, that's where they got yes and they got to there.
Adam: This train goes really fast. It's got that many 10. Loads and loads of Os on there so that means the train goes really fast. Goes faster than an Escort.
Chris: Faster than Escort?
Adam: Yes it does 'cause Escorts only go like that and this train goes …
Alex: This train goes really fast and you won't catch up with it.

It would appear that the opportunity for play allows understandings to emerge which might not otherwise occur. Throughout the episode the children are in control of their discourse and are establishing their own meanings. They are also incorporating their knowledge of numbers to try to make sense of the timetables. These interpretations do not emerge in isolation but occur through peer interaction and the particular script they establish for the play. When Adam starts the episode with 'You going on that train 10410? You have to hold on tight 'cause that will go really fast. You have to take your flask', he is suggesting a theme based on previous experiences of trains and train travel. This is later taken up by the others when Chris refers to sleeping on a train and Alex to hot dinners being put on the train. The discourse emerges through a framework of their shared knowledge.

The script enables each child to develop their understandings of what the symbols on the timetables might be for. Although they are not all clear what the noughts might mean, they attempt what they think are logical explanations. Chris makes the closest guess based on his knowledge of what the timetable is used for when he says, 'It gets in at 1 o'clock'. Adam's attempt to explain the 10 is more related to his knowledge of cars and speedometers in 'loads and loads of Os on there so that means the train goes really fast'. Here, within the play, he is able to try out something which appears to him to be logical and, although at first questioned by Alex, it is used to continue the script when Alex says, 'This train goes really fast and you won't catch up with it'.

Vygotsky (1978) has argued for the importance of social interaction with more experienced members of society in guiding cognitive development. The 'scaffolding' which exists when a parent or teacher supports and extends a child's learning encourages them towards a higher level of understanding. Heath (1983) has shown the importance of such social interactions between adults and children. The collaboration between peers has not received so much attention and has been shown to be complex. Studies of group involvement in collaborative processes suggest that the cognitive benefits of grouping children to include more competent peers does not necessarily result in a higher level of understanding for those still in the zone of proximal development on the task (Tudge 1991). We perhaps need to look more carefully at the nature of the interaction which might be taking place as children collaborate with one another in their problem solving.

The children in the train sequence were much more equal partners in their collaboration in trying to make sense of the timetables. On several occasions they were scaffolding their learning for one another. In the example of the London cars, there is evidence of prior knowledge. One child remembers that cars sometimes go on a train to Scotland and tries to help the other understand that cars do not only go on a motorway. When Alex says 'But they can go on – so you are on the London, right at the back. Right at the top nearly and the rest is right at the top', he is attempting an explanation of something he has seen taking place and, although it is not clear, it is the beginnings of helping Adam to understand the concept.

Tharp and Gallimore (1988) provide further explanations of how this might occur in their model for progression through the 'zone of proximal development' (see Figure 5.3). Alex was attempting to provide assistance even though it was not

Recursive loop			
Capacity begins	Capacity developed		
Zone of proximal development			
Assistance from more capable others such as adults and other children	Assistance provided by the self	Internalising ideas. Performance fully developed	May forget some information and need to return to an earlier stage before moving forward
Stage 1	Stage 2	Stage 3	Stage 4

Figure 5.3 Progress through and beyond the ZPD
(Adapted from Tharp and Gallimore 1988)

understood. Although his idea was not fully developed, his discourse was a form of self- guidance that helped him to internalise his theory of the cars. He appeared to be in Tharp and Gallimore's second stage in which the child carries out a task without assistance from others but also without meaning that the performance or idea is fully developed; the child may need to return to this or the earlier stage before it is internalised.

There were also examples of disagreements, as in the example with the cars, with each following their own ideas within the script they had generated. Each child seemed to be working in their own 'zone of proximal development' which was influenced by their background culture, the script arising from the thematic context and the interactions with peers. These children had sufficient freedom in what they were able to do in the setting of the train station to encourage them to try out their mathematical understandings. These arose incidently and provided their teacher with information which might not otherwise have arisen.

Many play episodes arising in relation to literacy and numeracy emerge because children have absorbed sets of practices which are embedded in their culture. The analysis of such episodes often depends upon the demonstrations of functional experiences children are able to provide. Children who write birthday cards or letters to one another and post them are, as Hall has commented, 'part of a complex social process of affirming a special type of relationship with another human being' (Hall and Robinson 1995, p. 106). It is the embeddedness of activities within the culture which children are able to draw on which is frequently demonstrated in classroom experiences and in the examples we have provided.

Summary

In looking at both literacy and numeracy as it arises in play, it becomes clear that children can be helped to construct a mental world in which they are exploring their skills and understandings. Providing children with settings in which a complexity of events can take place means that they also need inputs and discussion to support their play. In many of the examples quoted in this chapter the play arose from carefully planned themes in which teachers were clear about the skills and knowledge they hoped would emerge in relation to literacy and numeracy. It was the freedom children were given to try things out for themselves which provided teachers with additional information on how ideas were being taken up and understood and insights on further teaching which might be required.

CHAPTER 6

Exploring History Through Play

So far our discussion has centred on children's immediate cultures and environments. We have explored how play can enhance children's understandings of their world and of their place and identity within it. In this chapter we aim to explore some of the ways in which children's understanding of the past can be enriched through play and how play activities can extend children's awareness of different cultures and social contexts.

The chapter begins with a case study describing young children playing in a Victorian laundry, and identifies opportunities for learning history. The relationship of play with the development of historical understanding is explored within the model of

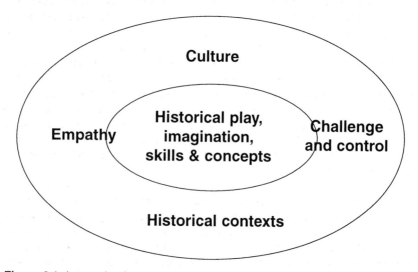

Figure 6.1 Interactive features of history through play

children's play outlined in Chapter 1. Further case-study material is used to demonstrate how play can enrich children's learning in history and enhance the development of historical skills and concepts. The creation by children of their own roles and identities is discussed and the role of the teacher in supporting children in their play is investigated. The chapter concludes with an evaluation of play as a means of developing historical understanding.

CASE STUDY

A Victorian laundry

Jane Fitzgerald, a final year student at the University of the West of England (UWE), planned a topic on homes for her Year 1 children and decided to organise a play area in a spare classroom as a Victorian laundry. The laundry was equipped with various artefacts, including a wooden dolly stick, a washboard, two galvanised tubs and a bucket, a wooden clothes horse, a wicker washing basket, three flat irons and a scrubbing brush. On one wall the children painted a fireplace with grate, glowing coals and a mantlepiece. An assortment of simple cotton garments was gathered together and hung on a clothes line stretching across the classroom with wooden clothes pegs. There was a variety of dressing-up clothes for the children to wear.

The children were encouraged to visit the laundry and to explore the different artefacts and clothes. Once they were familiar with the laundry, Jane began to discuss with the children some of the things they could see. Children began by thinking about the laundry cycle in their own home and then moved on to talk about washing in the past. They compared the artefacts in the play area with equipment which is used today. Initial thoughts about some of the artefacts were modified: children rejected earlier ideas that the dolly stick was a pogo stick or a clothes horse, and compared the effect of swishing clothes in a modern washing machine with the swishing achieved by the dolly in the tub.

What were the children learning as they talked and played in the laundry? They were acquiring information about past washing practices and becoming familiar with specific artefacts. The children were also learning that the past is different from the present; that as time passes, things change. The children had many opportunities to identify differences and changes in ways of life, and were also beginning to think about why things had changed. For example, one child explained that the Victorians needed to heat the irons beside the fire since they did not have electricity.

We would argue that these learning outcomes are very important. Nevertheless, they might have been achieved in other ways: by looking at pictures of Victorian laundries; visiting domestic collections in local museums or by inviting an older person to come into school to talk about how they used to launder their clothes in the past. Creating the play area, however, provided an added dimension to the children's learning experiences and enabled them to participate more fully in recreating a past way of life. The children were able to handle the artefacts, to experience their size and weight. As they did this, they began to appreciate how these artefacts were used and how they had impacted on people's lives, and so develop their own understandings of how people lived in the past. The arrival of the washing machine and tumble dryer has considerably reduced the amount of time spent washing clothes, while in the past doing the laundry was a long and arduous task – children were able to develop some awareness of this as they used the artefacts. 'It is hard work doing this' was mentioned frequently by different children as they used the dolly stick and scrubbing board and ironed the clothes in front of the fire.

The artefacts also provided a stimulus for children to create an identity for themselves centred on the past. Several children became completely absorbed in their tasks: one boy developed his ironing routine and didn't deviate from his practice of returning his flat iron to the fire to reheat as he ironed different garments. Another child became completely absorbed in the way she folded clothes into neat piles.

History and play

The above case study illustrates how children were able to recreate aspects of the past within their play. Returning to our original model, we can see how history, the story of past societies, can become part of the wider culture which impacts on children's play. Historical play offers a context for children's play which takes them beyond their immediate experiences to more distant times where they can encounter different ways of life. It introduces children to people's different values and beliefs and provides opportunities for exploring them in meaningful ways. As children play out their own versions of the past, not only do they develop their awareness of the different values, beliefs and ways of life of earlier societies, but they are also able to look afresh at their own place and current understandings of the contemporary world. Jane Fitzgerald, for example, found that the children had to revisit their current understanding of the present laundry cycle – what work does this involve? who does this work? does it take a long time? what machines are needed? and so on – to be able to appreciate the different stages involved.

Using their familiarity and understanding of modern laundry methods, children were challenged to extend their play with the Victorian artefacts. In this respect, as Cooper has observed, play gave the children the chance to 'make sense of what they have learned, to explore and develop it, and to integrate it with what they already know' (Cooper 1995, p. 64). Teacher intervention was important to provide an appropriate context and resources for the play. Yet the children were also very much in control of their play as they relived their present experiences within a Victorian society.

Learning history in the primary school

The case study demonstrates how play can contribute towards an understanding of the past. However, this might not always incorporate history. The History Working Group made the useful distinction between the 'past', i.e. everything which has ever happened, and 'history', a more critical study which seeks to explain and to investigate the past (DES 1990, p. 1). Historians have particular interests and ways of working; they are concerned with chronology and placing events and objects in temporal sequences. They identify changes as well as the continuous threads which link the past with the present, and run across different periods of time. They seek to explain why things happened and draw on a wide variety of evidence to support their explanations. The importance of developing such skills and concepts has remained prominent throughout the different versions of the history National Curriculum and have been incorporated within the Key Elements (DfE 1995) in the current history curriculum, together with the acquisition of particular historical knowledge.

The importance of a variety of sources such as artefacts, pictures and photographs, documents and maps, people talking about their own past, music and buildings and historical sites is emphasised in the National Curriculum. Using various sources we can begin to piece together different information about ways of life in the past. Often our story is incomplete; we can only base the story on the evidence which has been left behind. Often the story may vary, since sources can be interpreted in different ways and used as evidence by historians holding differing values and beliefs. However neutral we might attempt to be, inevitably our views of the past are coloured by our perceptions of the present. This is particularly noticeable in young children's work in history; they interpret sources within the light of their own, often limited, experiences. When the children were playing in the Victorian laundry with the Victorian artefacts, for example, there were many instances when they developed their existing conceptions of roles and routines within their play. They were not always playing at being Victorians!

Although it is difficult to shed our twentieth-century beliefs and values, if we are to grasp some understanding of the past and to identify with the people who lived in it, then it is important that we should attempt to appreciate their different viewpoints and to empathise with their different feelings. Drama and role play can provide many opportunities for children to enter into the past and to develop awareness of people's feelings and motivation. However, such ways of working could be seen as 'merely "dressing up" or "pretending" which, however valuable or enjoyable, is not necessarily sound history' (DES 1990, p. 177), and HMI warn against 'uncontrolled flights of the imagination' (DES 1988, p. 7). Good historical reconstructions and play are dependent on detailed knowledge and a respect for evidence.

Children need a range of historical knowledge to enable them to understand the context for their play and to provide authentic experiences. Such emphasis on authenticity is advocated by Wilson and Woodhouse (1990) and is prominent in Living History days organised at English Heritage sites (Fairclough 1994). The National Trust Youth Theatre also organises authentic reconstructions, providing opportunities for children to participate in everyday life in some of their properties, and also extending children's understanding by encouraging them to explore, in role, some of the issues which were important to people who lived at the time (Littlefair 1997).

Creating authentic historical reconstructions

Authentic reconstructions are dependent on the skill and knowledge of the teacher. Teachers' grasp of subject knowledge has been explored in the work of Shulman (1986), and is particularly in evidence in the current National Curriculum for teacher training (DfEE 1998). In the case of history, John (1991) identified different aspects of teachers' subject knowledge. He suggested teachers' historical knowledge included both personal knowledge of history and knowledge of how to teach history. Different strands within teaching history knowledge were:

- pedagogical content knowledge: knowledge of various approaches and strategies to teaching history;
- curriculum knowledge: knowledge of relevant texts and materials;
- organisational knowledge: knowledge about organising classroom learning.

This model of subject knowledge and its application in the classroom underpins the work of trainee history teacher students at UWE on their professionally related subject studies course. Professionally related subject studies enable students to link their academic studies in a specialist subject with work with children in school.

Each year it has become practice for first-year historians at the university to stage an event and organise a range of activities for a group of visiting primary school children on an historic theme. In recent years the themes which have been developed have ranged over a variety of historical periods: the Ancient Greeks; the visit of Queen Victoria to Bristol; the Aztecs; the burial of Queen Hatsheput, an Egyptian Pharaoh; a banquet to celebrate the Armada; the burial of an Anglo Saxon king (Kimber *et al.* 1995). Preparations begin with the students researching the historical period at their own level before being asked to consider how to make the information accessible to children.

CASE STUDY

John Cabot (II)

In 1997 students joined in the celebrations to commemorate the five hundredth anniversary of John Cabot crossing the Atlantic to Newfoundland. They researched aspects of medieval Bristol and the life of John Cabot, and became familiar with both primary and secondary source material. In order to make the information accessible to children, the students decided to enact the visit of Henry VII to Bristol in 1486, as described by an anonymous chronicler in the account, 'A Short and Brief Memory of the First Progresse of our Soveraigne King Henry VII' (McGraph 1985). The children followed Henry VII's procession through Bristol using a late Tudor map copied on to an overhead transparency.

Students acted the part of Henry, various Bristol dignitaries, and Bristol merchants who presented a petition to Henry, asking for the restoration of trade. The children were involved as medieval Bristol citizens and a variety of activities was planned to enable them to appreciate life at the time. They learned to sing some Latin plainsong; they looked at different coats of arms and designed their own. They smelled the different spices available in the fifteenth century and recorded their provenance on 'old' (coffee-stained) maps of the world. Materials were dyed using various vegetable dyes and the children followed authentic recipes to make honey and cinnamon toast. The afternoon concluded with an interpretation of Cabot's departure for the New World, based on a painting in the Bristol City Museum and Art Gallery.

Throughout the day, the students encouraged the children to reflect on the past, encouraging questions such as: How do we know? Is this likely to have happened? Why might people have felt like this and have acted in this way? Children were shown the source materials from which the students had based their enactments and different activities. As they were involved in these activities the children not only increased their knowledge of life in medieval Bristol but also developed an awareness that this knowledge is very dependant on the sources which have survived. For the students, the Cabot day provided opportunities for them not only to extend their own subject knowledge but also to develop their knowledge of teaching history.

In terms of our model of learning through play, the Cabot day provided structured opportunities for children to participate in an historical re-enactment. A less structured approach is evident in the case study below where children were encouraged to develop their own play, following specific historical input from student teacher, Ysanne Chivers.

CASE STUDY

The Viking ship: extending children's cultural experiences

Ysanne was interested in observing the extent to which Year 1 and 2 children were able to identify and learn about the distant past. She planned a series of activities over a half-term period to introduce the children to the Vikings and their ways of life. The sequence of activities provided the children with historical information which they were then asked to reorganise within a writing activity which was to contribute to a Viking newspaper. The activities included the following:

1. Brainstorming to establish children's existing perceptions of the Vikings. An introduction to the Vikings – who they were, where they lived and some of the things they did.
2. Finding information about Viking ways of life – food and farming, clothes, different jobs. Children thought of a list of things to take on a voyage.

3. Finding out how Viking ships were built – finding pictures of archaeological remains and reconstructions and weapons. Children were encouraged to write an extract from the ship's log.
4. Finding out about the Viking voyages and raids on Britain. The children wrote a letter home describing what they had been doing.
5. Finding further information about Viking ways of life – entertainment, jewellery and crafts, Viking gods. Children wrote an adventure story about the Vikings.

Ysanne also created a Viking ship to enable the children to extend their understanding of Viking ways of life through play. It was a splendid model with a gold painted dragon prow and a sail hoisted on a mast which could be lowered up and down. It was equipped with four oars and decorated shields hung over the sides. The children were thrilled with the ship and enjoyed playing in it. One group of children chose their own Viking names and Ysanne observed them closely at weekly intervals as they played in the ship.

As the children played in their Viking ship they established their own identities and drew on knowledge they had about Viking ways of life. They enjoyed pushing the boat off from the shore, ensuring that the oars were kept up and rowing off into the sea to fight and to get treasure. The children played a 'jump the oars' game which the Vikings actually played as they dared each other to jump from one oar to another without falling into the sea. Other incidents revealed that they were gaining familiarity with other aspects of Viking life: 'Look, there's another Viking boat. Let's put up the shields,' yelled one child, aware of the preparations needed for a potential battle. They passed around dried fish as a source of sustenance. As the weeks passed, Ysanne noted that the children included more details about Viking ways of life in their play and, at times, the children appeared to appreciate how people might have felt at the time. With their body movements, they demonstrated how tiring it was to row for a long period of time, and they swayed and rocked about as storms and bad weather interrupted their voyage.

There was also some evidence that children were able to support each other in their historical learning as they worked together to establish historical accuracy. For example, while the children were playing on the Viking ship, Michael the Mighty suggested that there was glue on their shields, but Bryony the Bry corrected him by saying, 'they didn't have no such thing then'. Similarly, Emily the Excellent corrected Bryony's insistence that the boat needed polishing by explaining, 'you don't get polish then'.

While the children did demonstrate some ability to empathise with the past and to appreciate past ways of life, they also maintained some current stereotypes. Gender distinctions, for example, were closely upheld. In the first play session, the boat landed and the two boys disembarked while the girls stayed behind and were exhorted by their leader, Michael the Mighty: 'Ladies, ladies, when they come put up your shields, up like this.' The girls were not allowed to disembark in the second play session either. Dino the Mighty Dragon said, 'Me and Michael see if it's safe on the land and you wash the clothes.' The girls complied and began to wash the clothes until Emily the Excellent decided that she had had enough and picked up an axe and shield. She was soon put in her place, however, when Michael the Mighty noticed – 'No you have to do the washing', to which Emily replied that they had already done it and carried on pretending to fight.

People in the past: creating an identity

In the examples of the Victorian laundry and the Viking ship we have shown how young children responded to an imaginative role-play situation; they created their own roles and identities, weaving them around different resources provided by the teacher and their developing knowledge of the historical period. As children grow older they are able to research more information for themselves and to investigate areas which they find personally interesting. Browsing through different history books can be an interesting and fruitful way to begin an historical topic. A group of history specialist students began to do this and looked through a variety of books about Ancient Egypt, selecting information which they found personally interesting to share with their colleagues. A range of information was gathered in a group brainstorm.

However, to focus their reading more sharply, the students were then requested to imagine that they were Ancient Egyptians and to draw and describe a character who might have lived at the Pharaoh's court. They had to give their characters a name and family identity as well as to provide descriptions of their work and leisure interests. With such a clear focus, the pace of the student's work changed rapidly; browsing and dipping into different books was replaced by referring to indices and chapter contents. Students identified specific information which they needed to find out to create their character. They raised questions which guided their researches. For example, one group of students imagined that they were an Egyptian dancer. They began to ask questions such as:

- What instrument would I play?
- What costume would I wear?
- When would I dance?
- What would be my age?

Another group of students imagined that they were employed to keep a Pharaoh cool – they wanted to find out about the fan man! Questions which interested them included:

- What was his background like?
- Was he rich or poor?
- Was there a ranking among slaves?
- Do you think he was a body guard as well as a fan man?
- Do you have to be the fan man once you reach a certain age?
- Were slaves allowed to marry?
- Would he be barefoot?
- How much spare time does he get?

Answers could not be found to all these questions (which once again reveals how much our knowledge of the past is dependent on available sources of information – if the sources are incomplete or do not exist we can only surmise what could have happened or what the past was like).

The creation of individual identities is also important since it emphasises the point that history is essentially about people with different roles and places in society. These people actually lived and had their own thoughts and emotions, their own preoccupations and interests. If we are to understand the past we need at least to try to appreciate the feelings, values and beliefs which inspired and motivated them to act in the ways they did.

This can be achieved, although not without difficulty. Controversy surrounds the extent to which we are able to empathise with people in the past (Jenkins and Brickley 1989; Low-Beer 1989). Our feelings and views are influenced by our experience in the twentieth-century world and we can never fully get a grasp of everything relating to a past society: 'Men and women in the past cannot be brought back to life. Their experiences cannot occur again' (Campbell and Little 1989, p. 34). But if we are to understand the past, we do need to exercise our imagination and develop some appreciation of people's feelings, what interested them, and what motivated them to act as they did. The following case study illustrates this point of view further.

CASE STUDY

Sharing feelings and beliefs

Jennie Brislen was reading the book *A Parcel of Patterns* by Jill Paton Walsh to her class of Year 5 and 6 children. The story is based on actual events occurring in the remote Derbyshire village of Eyam in 1665. A tailor, who had ordered cloth from London where the plague was raging, contracted the disease and died. The plague spread rapidly through the village. Rather than run away the villagers decided to isolate themselves from the rest of the world to prevent the infection from spreading. In the 15 months which the plague took to run its course, nearly two-thirds of the villagers perished.

As she was reading the story, Jennie encouraged the children to consider what it would have been like to have lived in Eyam at the time of the plague. The children were asked to create a character from one of the inhabitants and to write down their feelings about the plague. The following examples reveal how children were able to project themselves into the feelings of people living at the time and adopt their perspectives:

> I felt really bad that I might be the last person in the village or this might be my last minute or even my last second. Nearly every door in the village had a cross on it. There was difficulty and worry as I go to get water because on the way I might catch the plague. I hope that I never will get the plague and nobody else.

> There is a plague in our village. I feel locked up. Not being able to see anyone in case I pass it on. I have no idea whether I have it or not, but I am just being on the safe side. I'm scared. I don't know what to do. I wish we could just have a normal life. People are dying everywhere.

Once the children had established their identities and thought through their feelings they were asked to make some decisions. They had to decide whether to leave the village and risk spreading the disease or whether to remain at Eyam with the likelihood of death. As the children considered their decisions, they listened to different points of view and carefully constructed their own arguments from the range of historical information available to them.

The general feeling of the villagers was summarised by one child: 'We are not happy here because there is a smell of death around us. Our children will die of grief if we stay.' Yet ultimately the villagers decided to stay within the village. The decision to remain in the village was a painful one and the children were able to experience some of that pain and identified with some of the misery as they discussed what they should do in their roles as villagers.

Children learning together: developing their own scripts and interactions

In this chapter we have discussed history's influence in widening children's cultural experiences and explored children's versions of the past and the support which teachers can provide. We now turn to consider ways in which children can support each other and create their own scripts in play activities.

In the Viking ship the children initially pursued their own individual play agenda and largely ignored the contributions from other members of their group. However, as the weeks progressed they began to become more aware of each others' different roles. During the first play session Dino the Mighty Dragon exclaimed, 'Hurry up, we're not gonna land yet, there's a storm coming. We are all wet and cold and I've catched a cold.' His comments, however, were largely ignored by the other children. The following week Dino returned to the storm theme and explained that they had hit high winds. He rocked and swayed and this time his actions were copied by two other children, one of whom fell out of the boat. From the third play session onwards all the children then became involved in the storm, getting thrown about the boat, trying to row, ensuring that the sail was up and rescuing anyone who fell overboard.

At times, to maintain the action, children came out of their role so that they could tell the others what they should be doing: 'you sail back to our home and leave me on the island,' Dino instructed before he returned to being a Viking once more.

In the plague story children selected an incident to act out. They talked and listened to each other and gave instructions as they proceeded with the drama. At times, children were critical of each others' performances. For example one child scorned the portrayal of the scene of the tailor's deathbed; the child who was acting as the tailor's landlady was not projecting her emotions fully: 'Don't be stupid. She wouldn't just stand ... She'd be crying like this ... *(demonstration)* ... do this *(child puts her hands to her face and pretends to weep)*.

The value of play in learning history

The case-study material in this chapter reveals the many opportunities which play affords for learning history. Other research, too, has indicated how drama activities can enhance children's learning. Goalen and Hendry (1993) found that children's test scores improved markedly following a series of lessons and drama activities linked with learning about the Aztecs. The improvement in their scores contrasted with those scores from children in a control class who experienced the same lessons but did not participate in any drama activities.

Children also recognise how effective drama and play can be in helping them to learn. As Dino the Mighty Dragon explained:

> Miss 'cause when you write you can show it to people and you can remember what you done after you write but in the Viking boat, in the boat you can remember what you've done but you can't show people 'cause you don't write it, but you learn.

All the children on the Viking boat recognised how play had enhanced their learning and enabled them to remember more than when they were asked to write. Emily the Excellent explained that playing in the boat was effective since:

> in the boat you can move round 'cause like it's really happening. Well you're pretending but it's really happening really to you. When you are writing down it's not really happening to you at that time.

Similar views were expressed by children involved in the Cabot day, and many children acknowledged that the play and different activities had actually developed their understanding of medieval life further:

> It is much more fun than reading and it's easier to understand.

> I think it was nice to learn about so much more and instead of actually reading all those things in a book we actually did them. It was great fun and I learned a lot.

> I think it was very enjoyable because you actually did things and learned together at the same time. Instead of looking at books and writing which gets boring after a while.

Conclusion

Three characteristics for good learning in history are suggested by Fines and Nichol (1997): 'it must excite and entice children and be theirs, it must be true and honour the past, it must leave you understanding yourself and the present a lot better'. This chapter has attempted to describe some of the ways in which this might be achieved. Such opportunities for play and drama need to be particularly emphasised within the current educational context. Education Secretary David Blunkett's January 1998 announcement concerning the suspension of the statutory requirements to teach the foundation subjects could potentially reduce the amount of time allocated to teaching history in schools. A consequence of this reduction may be the diminution of opportunities for historical play and drama in the classroom. We need to be clear about the educational opportunities which such play presents so that we can argue for its establishment and maintenance within the curriculum.

Summary

This chapter has sought to describe how children's experience and understanding of less familiar contexts and cultures can be developed through play centred on ways of life in the past. We have discussed the contribution which play can make to children's historical understanding as well as to an understanding of their own values and the contemporary world. The importance of detailed historical knowledge and a respect for evidence has been emphasised to encourage children to empathise with people living in the past and to experience authentic reconstructions of past ways of life. The chapter has stressed the important role for teachers in providing appropriate contexts and resources for children to develop their play. Play activities provide particularly imaginative and interesting ways to learn about the past and this chapter has urged teachers to plan for such activities as they develop their curriculum in the future.

CHAPTER 7

Constructing the Social World: From Play into Drama

Throughout this book we have been promoting the idea that opportunities for classroom play can enable children to explore their imaginative experiences freely. We have shown that where role-play themes are part of classroom experiences children have freedom to try out their knowledge in their own way. In this chapter we turn to how role and dramatic play can gradually become more formalised as drama. We go on to show how there are opportunities for role play and drama within the statutory framework and ways in which drama can be developed in each Key Stage.

While dramatic play enables children to take on roles and play them out as ongoing improvisations, drama is more stylised in the use of techniques and is more of an interpretation of a particular event or story. It can also be in the form of a performance to others. Figure 7.1 shows the move from discourses of role and dramatic play to the more focused discourses of drama.

In dramatic play children are still very much in the 'as if' stage where they can be natural and imaginative in the way the play will develop. The episodes of play are also very open ended, often despite the structures which may have arisen within the classroom context. In many of our examples where children have played within a play theme, they have still made the play their own and explored imaginative ideas spontaneously. We associate drama more with the structured activities which encourage actions, intonations, and the use of particular scripts to develop

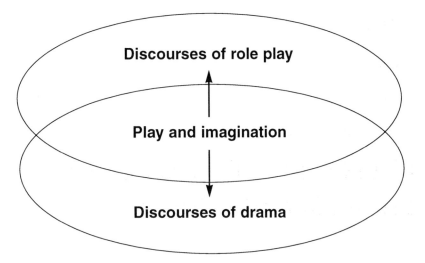

Figure 7.1 Links between role play and drama

aspects of speaking and listening. The other aspect of drama that is important to remember is that it can unite children in cooperating on a focused task.

Role play and drama in the statutory requirements

If we consider the requirements for play and talk which are suggested in fulfilling the Desirable Outcomes for the under-fives:

- Personal and Social Development involves cooperation and taking turns, showing initiatives, engaging in spontaneous role play and showing concentration and perseverance;
- Language and Literacy involves taking part in role play, making up stories and recognising patterns and rhymes;
- Creative Development mentions opportunities for using imagination as part of role play. (SCAA 1996, pp. 2–5)

This kind of check list is almost spurious when we consider the richness which is so often apparent in the play opportunities which can be made available in early years settings. What does emerge is that imaginative play activities can be a basis for developing a range of skills which extend children's overall development.

Teachers in primary schools also encourage children's speaking and listening skills through role play and drama. In the National Curriculum English requirements for Key Stage 1, children need to have opportunities to talk for a range of purposes, including:

- telling stories, both real and imagined;
- imaginative play and drama;
- exploring, developing and clarifying ideas, predicting outcomes and discussing possibilities;
- giving reasons for opinions and actions.

> Pupils should be encouraged to participate in drama activities, improvisations and performances of varying kinds, using language appropriate to the role or situation. They should be given opportunities to respond to drama they have watched, as well as that in which they have participated. (DfEE 1995, p. 4)

At Key Stage 2 the range of activities includes:

> improvisation, role play, and the writing and performance of scripted drama. In responding to drama they should be encouraged to evaluate their own and others' contributions.

In terms of standard English and language study:

> pupils should be taught to use an increasingly varied vocabulary ... through activities that focus on words and their meanings including language used in drama, role play and word games.
>
> This includes the skills of listening to others and clarifying meanings; recalling and representing important features of argument, talk, presentation, reading, radio and television programmes. They should qualify or justify what they think after listening to other opinions and accounts and deal politely with opposing views. (DfE 1995, p. 11)

When we consider the National Curriculum requirements for English for Key Stages 1 and 2 we realise just how much is covered in the role and dramatic play and the drama which occurs in primary classrooms. This is not lost in the requirements for the National Literacy Strategy (DfEE 1998) which provides opportunities for role play and drama in the text level work identified for both Key Stages. In Year 1, Term 2 there are statements as follows:

8. To identify and discuss characters e.g. appearance, behaviour, qualities; to speculate about how they might behave; to discuss how they are described in the text, and to compare characters from different stories and plays.

9. To become aware of character and dialogue e.g. by role playing parts when reading stories and plays with others. (DfEE 1998, pp. 22–3)

In Year 4, Term 1 are the following requirements:

5. To prepare, read and perform playscripts, comparing organisation of scripts with stories – how are settings indicated and story lines made clear.

6. To chart the build up of a play scene e.g. how scenes start, how dialogue is expressed, and how scenes are concluded. (DfEE 1998, pp. 38–9)

In Year 5, Term 1:

5. To understand dramatic conventions including:
the conventions of scripting (e.g. stage directions as asides);
how character can be communicated in word and gesture;
how tension can be built up through pace, silences and delivery. (DfEE 1998, pp. 44–5)

All of these requirements give much scope for using and encouraging dramatic role play and drama as part of classroom life and in encouraging children to build up knowledge about the skills required for characterisations and dramatic presentations.

We should also bear in mind that drama is an art form in its own right and be encouraging children to appreciate this: 'The ability to use [an artform] as a vehicle for expression is in large measure a learned ability and the teacher has a much more complex task than simply providing materials and encour- agement' (E. Eisner, quoted in Booth 1994, p. 27).

As a result, the teacher is much more involved in the activity of structuring the opportunities for children to appreciate their experiences. This is a very subtle development, particularly for younger children, and one which teachers need to plan for quite carefully if children are to continue to develop and include their own ideas.

It is through dramatic play developing into drama that children begin to understand the structure in acting out an episode, and to know about performance and audience. As we showed in our discussion of scripting, young children's knowledge of structure may be emerging intuitively as they incorporate their experience of events and stories into their play. As they begin to take on the form and dramatise it as a performance, the drama aspects of the activity are being developed. That is not to say that all imaginative play is always moving towards such a goal, but it frequently becomes more structured as children use their 'what if' activities as a preliminary to a performance. Children are learning to create drama and polish and refine how they put it across. They are also learning the conventions of different dramatic forms as they relate to other cultures and historical events.

A group of teachers in Coventry put together their aims in developing drama within the curriculum:

The teacher will aim to help pupils:
1. to work collaboratively in a range of group situations (e.g. friendship groups and teacher directed groups).
2. to work in role expressing ideas, thoughts and feelings that enable them to understand and empathise with a range of situations, some of which involve different points of view.
3. to develop social skills through devised drama in groups and explore issues beyond their immediate experiences.
4. to think more consciously and deeply about the world around them.
5. to develop a greater awareness and appreciation of the world in which they live.
6. to be involved in the processes of devising, planning and putting on a performance.
7. to be involved in a range of performance styles (e.g. mime, scripted plays, improvisations).
8. to develop performance skills by creating opportunities for them to present prepared and rehearsed pieces to an audience.
9. to watch or experience a range of performances (e.g. film, live radio).
10. to respond with critical awareness to a watched performance.
11. to have understanding of the dramatic and theatrical traditions of other cultures, societies and times. (City of Coventry Education Service 1996, p. 4)

We give these aims in full because they capture the essence of the move to dramatic mode that teachers work towards as they develop the possibilities within children's imaginative play in a more patterned way. This is not, however, to deny the spontaneity and expression which children may bring to their dramatic activities.

From play to drama in early years classrooms

The social contexts in which dramatic and sociodramatic play may occur can vary within classroom settings according to the physical spaces and resources which are available. The learning contexts suggested in *The Primary Language Record* (Barrs *et al.* 1988) include play, dramatic play, drama and storying. These may occur when children are working in pairs, in a small group, with an adult or in a larger group with an adult. The matrix in Figure 7.2 is useful for identifying and checking children's experiences in the classroom and monitoring the opportunities on offer.

Sometimes it is important to encourage pair work so that children can work on particular aspects of a theme of play, and it does encourage both children to develop their conversation skills. Marian Oughton (1997), a freelance storyteller, describes storytelling with nursery children, encouraging them to share their favourite stories with a partner. Although it took a while to organise, the children soon became involved and began to appreciate the need to listen as well as talk. In a story she told to the children, they were able to take control of parts of it through talking with their partners:

> For instance, they decided with their partners as the story progressed, how to catch the blackbird, what clothes to take on the journey, how to rescue the blackbirds from prison. Finally each pair made up their own endings for the story. (Oughton 1997, p. 9)

In planning for the transition from play into drama there are many opportunities for helping children to think about their play and the actions and conversations taking place. Where a role-play area has been established with an identified theme it is valuable

	Social contexts			
Learning contexts	Pair	Small group	Child with adult	Small or large group with adult
Drama in a storytelling session				
Dramatic play in a role-play area				
Informal writing as a part of dramatic play				
Using storyboards to develop a story				
Construction as part of a class theme				

Figure 7.2 Opportunities for talking and listening (adapted from Barrs *et al.* 1988, p. 38)

to focus on the dramatic aspects of what may be happening through:

• setting the scene;
• dressing-up clothes;
• actions (sometimes associated with music/movement);
• getting into roles – empathy.

In *setting the scene* teachers may discuss with children the kinds of artefacts and arrangements that could be part of the role-play area. This might include children bringing appropriate objects from home and drawing plans of how the area might be set up. Children often find storyboards useful in making characters or scenes and moving them around as required. This involves planning and organisation and making decisions cooperatively about what might be the best way to develop the play.

Dressing-up clothes can also add to the reality of a play area by being appropriate to the theme. Sometimes children will bring these for themselves or may make or add to them depending on the needs of the play. It is particularly important that such items are culturally appropriate and realistic to support the play which is taking place.

Where the theme of the role play is based on a story or series of stories, engaging children in the *actions* that accompany it can encourage the role play and drama to develop. Children playing in the spaceship tried out the actions of being in a spacesuit and moving around the ship. Others on the ocean liner tried lifeboat drill. The role play to associated rhymes also helped to set the scene. Sometimes the use of music and movement lessons can add to character development by encouraging children to move in certain ways. Toys in a toy shop or 'Peter and the Wolf' can be developed very effectively in this way, wherever possible incorporating these other areas of the curriculum.

Thinking about how it feels to be *in role* requires a certain amount of empathy. Even when very young children are acting out they can be encouraged to develop empathy for the characteristics and characters they are trying to portray. Giving children a few moments to think how they would feel if they were angry, frightened, happy or sad enables them to participate in the acting in a more thoughtful way and helps others to appreciate the emotions which are part of the situation. We encourage empathy in many early years settings and in play it can emerge more naturally as children begin to put themselves into the role of their character. In the Ahlbergs' book *The Jolly Postman* there is a letter from Goldilocks which says, 'I am very sory indeed that I cam into your house and ate Baby Bears porij' – a feeling young children are able to enjoy and relate to in appreciating the emotions within the Three Bears story.

Many of the picture books available for children carry messages about emotions in very clever ways. Max in Sendak's *Where the Wild Things Are*, Shirley in John Burningham's *Come Away from the Water Shirley*, and Alfie in Shirlie Hughes' story *Alfie Gets in First* are all characters whose feelings children can appreciate. For older children, Catherine Storr's stories of Clever Polly and her conversations with the wolf are humorous and bring in all the other stories children have read about wicked wolves. All of these characters enable children to think 'what if' and to identify with how they might look and feel if they were engaged in the conversations.

Increasing children's involvement and concentration enables them to get into the mood of whatever theme they are in. It is worth spending time to show how movements, miming and pace can be used to create different effects. In a very simple drama based on the subject of The Toy Shop, for example, children took on the roles of different toys and worked on the movements for each one:

- the clockwork animals were jerky and moved in a mechanical way;
- the toy soldiers with drums had stiff, straight movements;
- the dolls danced;
- the bears were all shapes and sizes and wobbled about;
- the space people floated.

Once the children had tried out their movements they were ready to participate in the story in which the soldiers open all the boxes and let the toys out to play. When the shopkeeper returns the following morning he finds some of the toys in the wrong boxes and has to take them all out to be rearranged. When he is not looking they change places quickly or move their limbs very slowly. In the final episode the toys have a party in which they are all able to try out their movements. This very simple idea can include dialogue as children become familiar with the story and develop it as a performance.

Play into drama with junior age groups

Opportunities for role play and drama with older children can emerge in more sophisticated ways as they get into the role play and appreciate the characterisation and dilemmas which may occur. Once again the play mode is an important one for children to experiment with their characters or settings and spontaneously build up an idea of how a character might behave or the actions might take place. This freedom to explore the idea is helpful in building up children's empathy for situations or roles. Marion Oughton (1997) always knows her stories very well before she tells all or parts of them to children. Sometimes she jumps straight into the story and encourages children to create their version of the characters whose attributes she has described. Even before the story is underway she finds that many children are miming the actions of different characters in the story and continue with this as the story progresses. Geoff Readman (1996, p. 16) suggests three questions to ensure that children are in no doubt about their role: Who am I in this drama context? Where am I in this drama context? When is this drama taking place?

Any good story may be used for the purpose of role play and drama with children, but as Penelope Harnett has shown in Chapter 6, historical episodes can be particularly fruitful. The children who acted out being villagers in *The Parcel Of Patterns* by Jill Paton Walsh could answer all the above questions and were also able to interpret their characters in their own way. This kind of freedom within the structure of the story and the drama being acted out allows children to be imaginative with their ideas, language and feelings without any pressures. It does not matter if it does not first come off as they wish, they can try it out again.

A teacher of Year 3 children used role play to help them understand early civilisations. She reported:

> By using role play, the work became problem solving, the children became much more involved. There was a real effort to go beyond the superficial, and they developed a real empathy with their characters. In this particular project, superstitions collected orally from parents and grandparents became a powerful link with the people of the past.

The cooperative elements come as children begin to pull their dramas together and appreciate their parts in relation to others, as the children did in *Macbeth*. In the end, in all the performances described, the structure was there but there was also flexibility for children to work on their own imaginative interpretations. A class of eight-year-olds worked on the story of *Bill's New Frock* by Anne Fine (1978). Their amusement and enthusiasm for the characters led to much empathy with members of the opposite sex. When they also read Gene Kemp's story *The Turbulent Term of Tyke Tyler* there was much rich discussion on different roles and how they saw themselves in relation to other members of the class.

Lesley Hendy (1997) refers to the work of Morgan and Saxton (1991) who developed categories for the range of questions which might be asked of children within groups. These were as follows:

- *Category A: Questions which elicit information.* These draw out what is already known of both information and experience and establish appropriate procedures for the conduct of the work.
- *Category B: Questions which shape understanding.* These help teachers and pupils to fill in what lies between the facts and sort out, express and elaborate how they are thinking and feeling about the material.
- *Category C: Questions which press for reflection.* These go beyond the facts and demand intellectual and emotional commitment by challenging the individual to think critically and creatively.

In the role-play area established for the ocean liner children played in groups of five or six. They had been given a ticket for a journey and had to decide where each group would go based on the many travel brochures and pictures they had collected. One group decided they wanted to go to Antarctica, having seen television programmes of explorers in that area. They had also read about Captain Scott and this had caught their imagination. They began by deciding that they would be modern explorers and each have a role. The ocean liner would only be able to take them so far, then they would need a plane and snowmobiles. In working through the different aspects of their play the teacher made use of the questions identified by Morgan and Saxton.

In Category A children were asked where they were going, who they would be, how long it would take to get there and what route they would take? The children began to establish a plan for the things they needed to find out and where to get the information. Each character would talk about their role.

Category B questions were based on the temperatures they might expect, the kind of clothes the would need and how much weight they could carry. This went much further on from the original theme in terms of finding information and using it. It also encouraged different children to develop their specific interests, for example, one child was particularly interested in the wildlife and found out all about penguins and how to study them, to feed back to the others. The teacher also raised questions such as 'What would happen if …?' and 'How would you feel if …?'

In Category C the questions became more reflective, asking the children to develop a scenario in which they had to think of ways to help one another in a blizzard when the snowmobiles were frozen.

The level of empathy in the dramatic play episodes which emerged was much richer due to the explorations children had to make into the situations they might find themselves in. The play promoted many of the benefits we would hope would arise in such activities, including: challenge, control, creativity, improvisation, negotiation, collaboration, leadership skills, working as a team, turn taking, sharing, and learning to appreciate and use one another's expertise.

Strategies

The following are some of the strategies which might be used in encouraging children to think about their characters and the action in their drama sequences.

- *Still images:* the children freeze an action as in a photograph. They could try two or three to represent their play, for example: Mrs Grinling in the cottage preparing the basket; Mrs Grinling sending the basket on the rope; Mrs Grinling watching the basket reach the lighthouse. The children then add conversation or descriptions to the images.
- *Freeze frames:* several images tell an episode of the story. This might be done with pictures, paintings or a series of mimed, still photographs. They can then be put in the order of the episode or story. Another way of using freeze frames is for individuals to develop their role and write about themselves, elaborating their feelings about the kind of character they may be. They may be questioned on this by others in the group.
- *Pair work:* children tell one another about their favourite part of the story or the character they played. They might develop a conversation in role and then compare versions with another pair.

- *Hot seating:* individuals in role are asked to speak aloud their reactions to particular events in the story, for example, Mr Grinling swinging across to the lighthouse on a rope. They can be questioned by others while they are in role and also be asked what they feel about their role.

Encouraging children to explore challenging issues is an important aspect of drama with all children. It can help them to focus on the dilemmas which might occur in different situations, and self-confidence and social and interpersonal skills may be developed through these play opportunities. Dilemmas can arise from stories, historical or moral situations which make children consider their roles and how they might handle them.

David Booth (1994) suggests valuable strategies for developing drama which can also be easily assessed:

- responding to a story in role;
- improvisations in a group;
- interviewing;
- reporting on events;
- group tableaux;
- choral speaking;
- exploring through sound and dance, drama and mime.

These are all strategies which might be employed and related to classroom themes. Activities can be identified to promote these ideas, for example, in the work on *The Iron Man* an interviewing strategy was used to find out information from the owner of the scrap yard where the Iron Man went for his food. From tapes of children's discussions in the recording studio area and observations of the final interview, the teacher was able to record assessments based on this activity. She noted the way children built up the discussion, revealed their feelings in role, engaged in turn taking and responded to the ideas of others. Ensuring that children have the freedom to build up their scenarios, but also giving guidance through structures or questions, builds up fruitful experiences in appreciating dramatic conventions.

Summary

This chapter has provided some examples of the activities which can encourage children to take up styles of dramatic productions. In doing this they are making a jump from their imaginative role play to using imagination within a framework which requires specific language or actions to develop an idea or meaning. In such a framework there are opportunities for children not just to create appropriate language but to use it to solve specific problems or dilemmas which may have arisen within their own lives and culture, or be part of understanding other cultures and ways of life and behaviour. The discourses which arise in dramatic play become more focused as drama but continue to enable children to develop imaginative interpretations. This is an aspect of play which teachers can use to promote empathy and understanding across curriculum areas.

Conclusion

Throughout this book we have argued for the inclusion of imaginative play as part of the planning of activities within the curriculum. We have suggested that in many episodes of classroom play children are able to construct their own understandings of their experiences by engaging in pretend and role-play activities in thematic play areas.

The classroom context

Recently, one of us had two very different classroom experiences. The first was with four- and five-year-olds in a Reception class. A range of play activities were available for them at all times, including water, wet and dry sand, small world and construction as well as an imaginative role-play area set up as the Three Bears' cottage. This had been planned by the children and contained books, a telephone directory, junk mail and writing materials. They had decorated the area with paintings and written letters to Goldilocks. The opportunities for early writing, speaking and listening, art and music, were all available and taken on board with enthusiasm. The teachers in the school had no problems in covering the areas of learning or showing that children would be able to achieve the Desirable Outcomes by the age of five. Nor did they show concern about covering the different subject areas at Key Stage 1 for the five-year-olds. For them, play was an essential part of their planning in achieving their goals and in enabling children to learn from their experiences. So often this is not the case. Basic skills seem to predominate in the activities available to primary-aged children, leaving them little time to develop their understandings of the world through more imaginative experiences.

In the second setting, seven-year-olds were involved in a Literacy Hour. They began by looking at a big book on toys and using a contents page and index to find information. The children then went on to look at cards showing consonant blends and suggesting words beginning with the sounds. They then worked in four ability groups:

- making up words as part of the game of Scrabble and writing down the rules on a large sheet;
- making up more words using the consonant blends with the help of a teacher assistant;
- group reading with their teacher;
- choosing a toy and finding out more about it using small books based on the big book.

All of these activities were very focused and children participated in the whole hour with much enthusiasm. It ended with the teacher reviewing activities and some children offering rules for playing their game of Scrabble.

We offer these two examples because they typify different kinds of activities children may be engaged in during their school day. They are by no means mutually exclusive. While the first experience showed one aspect of classroom play, the second also included play in the form of a game. Because the Literacy Hour has a skills focus it is easy to see it as just that. Yet in looking at the topics included in big books, there are possibilities for also including imaginative play activities within the classroom environment to support the work emerging at text, sentence and word levels.

We should also bear in mind the intense nature of the structure of both the Literacy and Numeracy Hours. Children enjoy many of the activities and find them interesting, but the amount of concentration required by children each day is high and has to be sustained through the week. In acknowledging the value of play approaches we can include associated play activities within overall themes. In one school, a wildlife centre was set up where children could plan areas for birds and animals and decide on environments, appropriate food and amounts. This ran alongside the use of texts such as Martin Waddell's *Owl Babies*. Group activities could be planned within the thematic play area and allowed children to develop their skills in a relaxed way. In another class, a post office was set up to support phonic work introduced during the Literacy Hour. This again allowed young children that element of imaginary play which allowed them to try out the skills which had been introduced.

All this may sound like sitting on the fence. It is not! Building in opportunities for play in the structures which are now on offer is drawing on what we know are ways of enabling children to learn. If we are to be realistic about the demands on time in the primary classroom we have to appreciate where we are enabling children to use their creativity and imagination as well as their skills in an environment which promotes all those aspects of their development.

Although this sometimes seems difficult because of the poor press that play receives from parents and from society in general, we hope we have shown that it is the natural way in which children learn. It is also a means of enabling them to reflect upon the content of their activities and collaborate in sharing ideas. These many arguments for play will not be acceptable or convincing unless we as teachers believe them and are able to put them into practice and show their value in children's development and learning.

Julie Fisher (1996) suggests a charter for play which may support teachers in justifying it and planning for it across the curriculum:

1. Acknowledge its unique contribution as a process by which all children learn.
2. Plan for it as an integral part of the curriculum and not an 'added extra'.
3. Facilitate it with appropriate and high quality provision.
4. Act as a catalyst when intervention is appropriate and a scaffolder when expertise is required.
5. Observe it in order to have first hand evidence of children's learning.
6. Evaluate it in order to better understand the needs of the learner.

7. Value it through comment and commitment in order for its status in the classroom to be appreciated.
8. Fight for it with rigorous, professional arguments in order to bring about deeper understanding and acceptance by colleagues, parents, governors and the community at large. (Fisher 1996, p. 106)

To end this discussion it seems important to return to our opening comments about the classroom contexts in which teachers are working. We hope we have justified play as valuable in enabling children to extend their learning and utilise their experiences as they meet them. In no way do we deny the difficulties teachers have in balancing the curriculum to provide for all its demands. Yet if we believe in enabling children to make the most of their knowledge and imaginative ideas, we need to celebrate and promote the activities they engage in with success.

Bibliography

Anderson, A. and Stokes, S. (1984) 'Social and institutional influences on the development and practice of literacy', in Goelman, H., Oberg, A., Smith, F. (eds) *Awakening to Literacy*. Oxford: Heinemann.

Anning, A. (1991) *The First Years in School*. Buckingham: Open University Press.

Athey, C. (1990) *Extending Thought in Young Children: A Parent–Teacher Partnership*. London: Paul Chapman Publishing.

Barrs, M., Ellis, S., Hester, H., Thomas, A. (1988) *The Primary Language Record: A Handbook for Teachers*. London: ILEA/Centre for Language in Primary Education.

Bateson, G. (1955) 'A theory of play and fantasy', in Bruner, J., Jolly, A., Sylva, K. (eds) *Play: Its Role in Development and Evolution* (1976), 119–29. Harmondsworth: Penguin.

Beardsley, G. (1988) 'No, I'm the draw master', in Meek, M., Mills, C. (eds) *Language and Literacy in the Primary School*. Hove: The Falmer Press.

Bennett, N. (1976) *Teaching Styles and Pupil Progress*. London. Open Books.

Bennett, N., Wood, L., Rogers, S. (1997) *Teaching Through Play: Teachers' Thinking and Classroom Practice*. Buckingham: Open University Press.

Board of Education (1931) *Report of the Consultative Committee on Education on the Primary School* (The Hadow Report 1931). London: HMSO.

Board of Education (1933) *Report of the Consultative Committee on Education on the Infant and Nursery School* (The Hadow Report 1931). London: HMSO.

Booth, D. (1994) *Story Drama: Reading, Writing and Role Playing Across the Curriculum*. Markham, Ontario: Pembroke Publishers.

Bruce, T. (1991) *Time to Play in Early Childhood Education*. London: Hodder & Stoughton.

Bruner, J. (1996) *The Culture of Education*. Cambridge, Mass.: Harvard University Press.

Bruner, J. and Haste, H. (1987) *Making Sense: The Child's Construction of the World*. London: Methuen.

Bruner, J., Jolly, A., Sylva, K. (1976) *Play: Its Role in Development and Evolution*. Harmondsworth: Penguin.

Caldwell Cook, H. (1917) *The Play Way*. London: Heinemann.

Campbell, J. and Little V. (1989) *Humanities in the Primary School*. Hove: The Falmer Press.

Central Advisory Council for Education (England) (1967) *Children and their Primary Schools* (The Plowden Report). London: HMSO.

Christie, J. (ed.) (1991) *Play and Early Literacy Development*. New York: State University of New York Press.

City of Coventry Education Service (1996) *Drama in the Primary School*. Coventry: CCES.

Cochran Smith, B. (1984) *The Making of a Reader*. Norwood, NJ: Ablex Publishing.

Cooper, H. (1995) *History in the Early Years*. London: Routledge.

Cortazzi, M. (1993) *Narrative Analysis*. Hove: The Falmer Press.

Cox, C. B. and Boyson, R. (eds) (1975) *Black Paper 1975*. London: Dent.

Cox, C. B. and Boyson, R. (1977) *Black Paper 1977*. London: Temple Smith.

Csikszentmihalyi, M. (1979) 'The concept of flow', in Sutton Smith, B. (ed.) *Play and Learning*, 257–73. New York: Gardner Press.

Daiute, C. (1989) 'Play as thought: thinking strategies for young Writers', *Harvard Educational Review* 59(1), 1–23.

Daniels, J. (1994) 'You be de and I'll be de … Language, narrative and imaginative play', in Whitebread, D. (ed.) *Teaching and Learning in the Early Years*. London: Routledge.

Davis, A. and Pettitt, D. (eds) (1994) *Developing Understanding in Primary Mathematics. Key Stages 1 & 2*. Hove: The Falmer Press.

Dearden, R. (1968) *The Philosophy of Primary Education*. London: Routledge and Kegan Paul.

DES (1967) *Children and their Primary Schools*. London: HMSO.

DES (1988) *History from 5–16. Curriculum Matters 11*. An HMI Series. London: HMSO.

DES (1990) *National Curriculum History Working Group. Final Report*. London: HMSO.

DES (1990a) *Starting with Quality. The Report of Inquiry into the Quality of Educational Experiences Offered to 3 and 4 Year Olds* (The Rumbold Report). London: HMSO.

DfE (1995) *Key Stages 1 and 2 of the National Curriculum*. London: HMSO.

DfEE (1997) *Standards for the Award of Qualified Teacher Status*. London: HMSO.

DfEE (1998) *The National Literacy Strategy. Framework for Teaching*. London: HMSO.

Donaldson, M (1983) *Children's Minds*, 2nd edn. London: Flamingo.

Dunn, J. (1988) *The Beginnings of Social Understanding*. Oxford: Basil Blackwell.

Dyson, A. (1989) *The Multiple Worlds of Child Writers: Friends Learning to Write*. New York: Teachers College Press.

Edwards, D. and Mercer, N. (1987) *Common Knowledge*. London: Methuen.

Egan, K. (1988) 'The origins of imagination and the curriculum', in Egan, K. and Nadaner, D. *Imagination and Education*. Buckingham: Open University Press.

Fairclough, J. (1994) *A Teacher's Guide to History Through Role Play*. London: English Heritage.

Ferreiro, E. and Teberoski, A. (1983) *Literacy Before Schooling*. Oxford: Heinemann.

Fines J. and Nichol J. (1997) *Teaching Primary History*. Oxford: Heinemann.

Fisher, J. (1996) *Starting From the Child*. Buckingham: Open University Press.

Fox, C. (1993) *At the Very Edge of the Forest: The Influence of Literature on Storytelling by Children*. London: Cassell.

Fox, C. (1996) 'Children's conception of imaginative play revealed in their oral stories', in Hall, N. and Martello, J. (eds) *Listening to Children Think: Exploring Talk in the Early Years*. London: Hodder & Stoughton.

Froebel, F. W. (1826) *The Education of Man*. Trans. Heulman, W. N. New York: Appleton, 1887.

Gardner, D. (1969) *Susan Isaacs. The First Biography*. London: Methuen.

Goalen P. and Hendry L. (1993) 'It's not just fun, it works! Developing children's historical thinking through drama', *The Curriculum Journal* **4**(3), 363–79.

Goncu, A. (1987) 'Towards an interactional model of development changes in social pretend play', in Katz, L. (ed.) *Current Topics in Early Childhood Education* Vol. 7, 108–26. New York: Academic Press.

Goswami, U. and Bryant, P. (1990) *Phonological Skills and learning to Read*. Hillsdale, NJ: Lawrence Erlbaum.

Griffin, H. (1984) 'The co-ordination of meaning in the creation of shared make belief reality', in Bretherton, I. (ed.) *Symbolic Play*. New York: Academic Press.

Griffiths, R. (1994) 'Mathematics and play', in Moyles, J. (ed.) *The Excellence of Play*. Buckingham: Open University Press.

Gura, P. (ed.) (1992) *Exploring Learning: Young Children and Block Play*. London: Paul Chapman Publishing.

Hall, N. (1987) *The Emergence of Literacy*. London: Hodder & Stoughton.

Hall, N. and Abbott, A. (1991) *Play in the Primary Curriculum*. London: Hodder & Stoughton.

Hall, N. and Robinson, A. (1995) *Exploring Writing and Play in the Early Years*. London: David Fulton Publishers.

Halliday, M. (1975) *Learning How to Mean*. London: Edward Arnold.

Harste, J., Woodward V., Burke, C. (1984) *Language Stories and Literacy Lessons*. Oxford: Heinemann.

Haste, H. (1987) 'Growing into rules', in Bruner, J. and Haste, H. (eds) *Making Sense: The Child's Construction of the World*. London: Methuen.

Heath, S. (1983) *Ways With Words*. Cambridge: Cambridge University Press.

Hendy, L. (1994) 'It is only a story isn't it? Drama in the form of interactive story telling in the early years classroom', in Whitebread, D. (ed.) *Teaching and Learning in the Early Years*. London: Routledge.

Hendy, L. (1997) 'Drama. Talk in a new framework', *The Primary English Magazine* **2**(5), 20–23.

Higgins, E. T., Ruble D. N., Hartup, W. (1983) *Social Cognition and Social Development. A Sociocultural Perspective*. Cambridge: Cambridge University Press.

Hohmann, M. and Weikart, D. P. (1995) *Educating Young Children*. Ypsilanti, Mich.: High/Scope Foundation.

Jenkins, K. and Brickley, P. (1989) 'Reflections on the empathy debate', *Teaching History*, April, 18–23.

John P. (1991) 'The professional craft knowledge of the history teacher', *Teaching History*, July, 8–12.

Karrby, G. (1989) 'Children's conceptions of their own play', *International Journal of Early Childhood* **21**(2), 49–54.

Kimber, D., Clough, N., Forrest, M., Harnett, P., Menter, I., Newman, E. (1995) *Humanities in Primary Education*. London: David Fulton Publishers.

King, R. (1978) *All Things Bright and Beautiful: A Sociological Study of Infant Classrooms*. London: Wiley.

Kitson, N. (1997) 'Adult intervention in children's sociodramatic play', *Education 3–13*, March.

Klein, M. (1955) 'The psychoanalytic play-technique', *American Journal of Orthopsychiatry* **25**, 223–37.

Light, P. (1987) 'Taking roles', in Bruner, J. and Haste.H (eds) *Making Sense: The Child's Construction of the World*. London: Methuen.

Littlefair, S. (1997) 'The young National Trust theatre', *Primary History*, June, 13–14.

Low-Beer, A. (1989) 'Empathy and History', *Teaching History*, April, 8–12.

Lowenfeld, M. (1935) *Play in Childhood*. London: Gollancz.

Manning, K. and Sharp, A. (1977) *Structuring Play in the Early Years at School*. London: Ward Lock.

McGraph, P. (ed.) (1985) *Two Tudor Visits to Bristol. A Bristol Miscellany*. Bristol: Record Office.

Meek, M. (1991) *On Being Literate*. London: Bodley Head.

Morgan, N. and Saxton, J. (1991) *Teaching, Questioning and Learning*. London: Routledge.

Moyles, J. (1988) *Just Playing? The Role and Status of Play in Early Childhood Education*. Buckingham: Open University Press.

Moyles, J. (ed.) (1994) *The Excellence of Play*. Buckingham: Open University Press.

Murphy, P. and Elwood, J. (1997) 'The gender divide', research reviewed by Macleod, D., *Guardian Education*, 17 June.

Nelson, K. (1981) 'Social Cognition in a Script Framework', in Flavell, J. and Ross, L. (eds) *Social Cognitive Development: Frontiers and Possible Futures*. New York: Cambridge University Press.

Nelson, K., Seidman, S. (1984) 'Playing with scripts', in Bretherton, I. (ed.) *Symbolic Play*. New York: Academic Press.

Neuman, S. and Roskos, K. (1992) 'Literacy objects as cultural tools: effects on children's literacy behaviours in play', *Reading Research Quarterly* **27**(3), 202–35.

Oers, B. van (1994) 'Are you sure? Stimulating Mathematical Thinking During Young Children's Play', Paper for the Fourth European Conference on The Quality of Early Childhood Education. Goteborg, Sweden.

Oughton, M. (1997) 'Active storytelling in the early years', *Early Education*, Autumn, 8–9.

Paley, V. G. (1981) *Wally's Stories*. Cambridge, Mass.: Harvard University Press.

Pellegrini, A. (1984) 'Identifying causal elements in the thematic–fantasy play paradigm', *Americal Educational Research Journal* **21**, 691–703.

Pellegrini, A. and Galda, L. (1993) 'Ten years after: a re-examination of symbolic play and literacy research', *Reading Research Quarterly*, June, 163–73.

Piaget, J. (1962) *Play, Dreams and Imitation in Childhood*. London: Routledge and Kegan Paul.

Pollard, A. (1990) 'Towards a sociology of learning in primary schools', *British Journal of Sociology of Education* **11**(3), 241–56.

Pollard, A., Broadfoot, P., Croll, P., Osborn, M., Abbott, D. (1994) *Changing English Primary Schools? The Impact of the Education Reform Act at Key Stage 1.* London: Cassell.

Readman, G. (1996) 'Drama, imagination and feeling', *The Primary English Magazine* **1**(3), 22–5.

Roy, A. (1997) *The God of Small Things*. London: Flamingo.

School Curriculum and Assessment Authority (1996) *Nursery Education: Desirable Outcomes for Children's Learning on Entering Compulsory Education*. London: HMSO.

Shank, R. and Ableson, R. (1977) *Scripts, Plans, Goals and Understanding*. Hillsdale, NJ: Lawrence Erlbaum.

Shulman, L. (1986) 'Those who understand: knowledge growth in teaching', *Educational Researcher* **15**(2), 4–14.

Singer, D. and Singer, J. (1990) *The House of Make-Believe: Children's Play and the Developing Imagination*. Cambridge, Mass.: Harvard University Press.

Smilanski, S. (1971) 'Can adults facilitate play in children? Theoretical and practical considerations', in Smilanski, S. (ed.) *Play: The Child Strives Towards Self-realization*, 39–50. Washington, DC: NAEYC.

Smilansky, S. (1990) 'Sociodramatic play: Its relevance to behaviour and achievement in school', in Klugman, E. and Smilansky S. (eds) *Children, Play and Learning: Perspectives and Policy Implications*. Columbia: Teachers College, Columbia University.

Smilansky, S. and Shefatya, L. (1990) *Facilitating Play: A Medium for Promoting Cognitive, Socio-emotional and Academic Development in Young Children*. Gaithersburg, Md.: Psychosocial and Educational Publications.

Sutton Smith, B. and Kelly Bryne, D. (1984) 'The bipolarity in play theories', in Yawkey, T. D. and Pellegrini, A. D. (eds) *Child's Play: Developmental and Applied*. Hillsdale, NJ: Lawrence Erlbaum.

Tharpe, R. G. and Gallimore, R. (1988) *Rousing Minds to Life: Teaching, Learning and Schooling in Social Context*. Cambridge. Cambridge University Press.

Tudge, J. (1991) 'Vygotsky, the zone of proximal development and peer collaboration: implications for classroom practice', in Moll, L. (ed.) *Vygotsky and Education: Instructional Implications and Applications of Sociohistorical Psychology*. Cambridge: Cambridge University Press.

Vukelich, C. (1993) 'Play: a context for exploring the functions andfeatures of writing with peers', *Language Arts* **70**, 386–92.

Vygotsky, L. (1978) *Mind in Society: The Development of Higher Psychological Processes*. Cambridge, Mass.: Harvard University Press.

Walkerdine, V. (1982) 'From context to text: a psychosemiotic approach to abstract athought', in Beveridge, M. (ed.) *Children Thinking Through Language*. London: Edward Arnold.

Weininger, O. (1988) '"What if" and "as if" imagination and pretend play in early childhood', in Egan, K. and Nadaner, D. (eds) *Imagination and Education*. Buckingham: Open University Press.

Whitebread, D. (ed.) (1994) *Teaching and Learning in the Early Years*. London: Routledge.

Whitbread, N. (1972) *The Evolution of the Nursery–Infant School*. London: Routledge & Kegan Paul.

Wilson, V. and Woodhouse, J. (1990) *History through Drama. A Teachers' Guide*. Teaching History Serie,s No. 65. London: The Historical Association.

Wood, D. (1988) *How Children Think and Learn*. Oxford: Basil Blackwell.

Wood, E. and Attfield, J. (1996) *Play, Learning and the Early Childhood Curriculum*. London: Paul Chapman Publishing.

Children's books

Ahlberg, J. and Ahlberg, A. (1996) *The Jolly Postman and Other People's Letters*. London: Heinemann.

Armitage, R. and Armitage, D. (1985) *The Lighthouse Keeper's Lunch*. Harmondsworth: Puffin.

Armitage, R. and Armitage, D. (1986) *The Lighthouse Keeper's Catastrophe*. Harmondsworth: Puffin.

Armitage, R. and Armitage, D. (1989) *The Lighthouse Keeper's Rescue*. Harmondsworth: Puffin.

Burningham, J. (1977) *Come Away From the Water Shirley*. London: Collins Picture Lions.

Carle, E. (1972) *The Very Hungry Caterpillar*. Harmondsworth: Puffin.

Fine, A. (1989) *Bill's New Frock*. London: Mammoth.

Kemp, G. (1972) *The Turbulent Term of Tyke Tyler*. Harmondsworth: Puffin.

Hughes, S. (1981) *Alfie Gets in First*. London: Collins Picture Lions.

Hughes, T. (1966) *The Iron Man*. London: Faber and Faber.

Paton Walsh, J. (1983) *A Parcel of Patterns*. Harmondsworth: Kestrel.

Sendak, M. (1967) *Where the Wild Things Are*. London: Bodley Head.

Storr, C. (1978) *Clever Polly and the Hungry Wolf*. London: Mammoth.

Waddell, M. (1992) *Owl Babies*. London: Walker Books.

Index